"Japanese Flowers" Coloring Book

All Artwork by

Cort Bengtson

Published by
Cort's Royal Ink Tattoo Company
Book Design and Layout by
Cort Bengtson

Copyright 2018
All images are on file with
The Library of Congress

ISBN-13: 978-1-948187-29-9

All of the art drawn within was done by
a tattoo artist with the tattoo sensibility
in mind.
This is a coloring book of japanese flowers.
The outline was done in a pretty thick
calligraphy style brush stroke, in a
20 % gray line.
The gray line allows the individual artist
a chance to do a very realistic rendering
or a tattoo artist the ability to practice thier
outlining by just tracing over the existing
20% gray line.
You can also use these outlines as is for real
tattoo clients. Just make the ouline a
little darker then add some wind bars
or finger waves and presto
instant half sleeve or more!

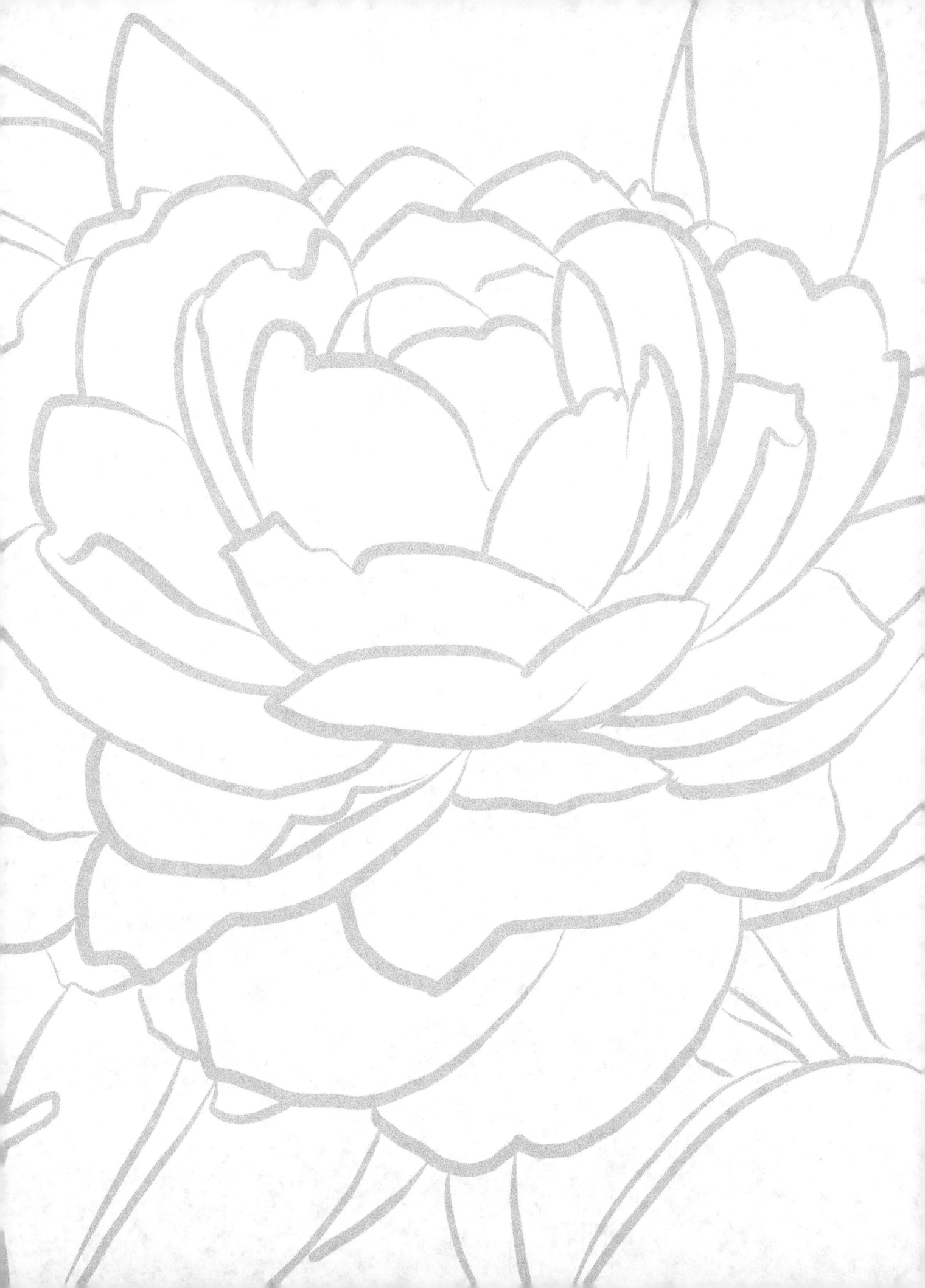

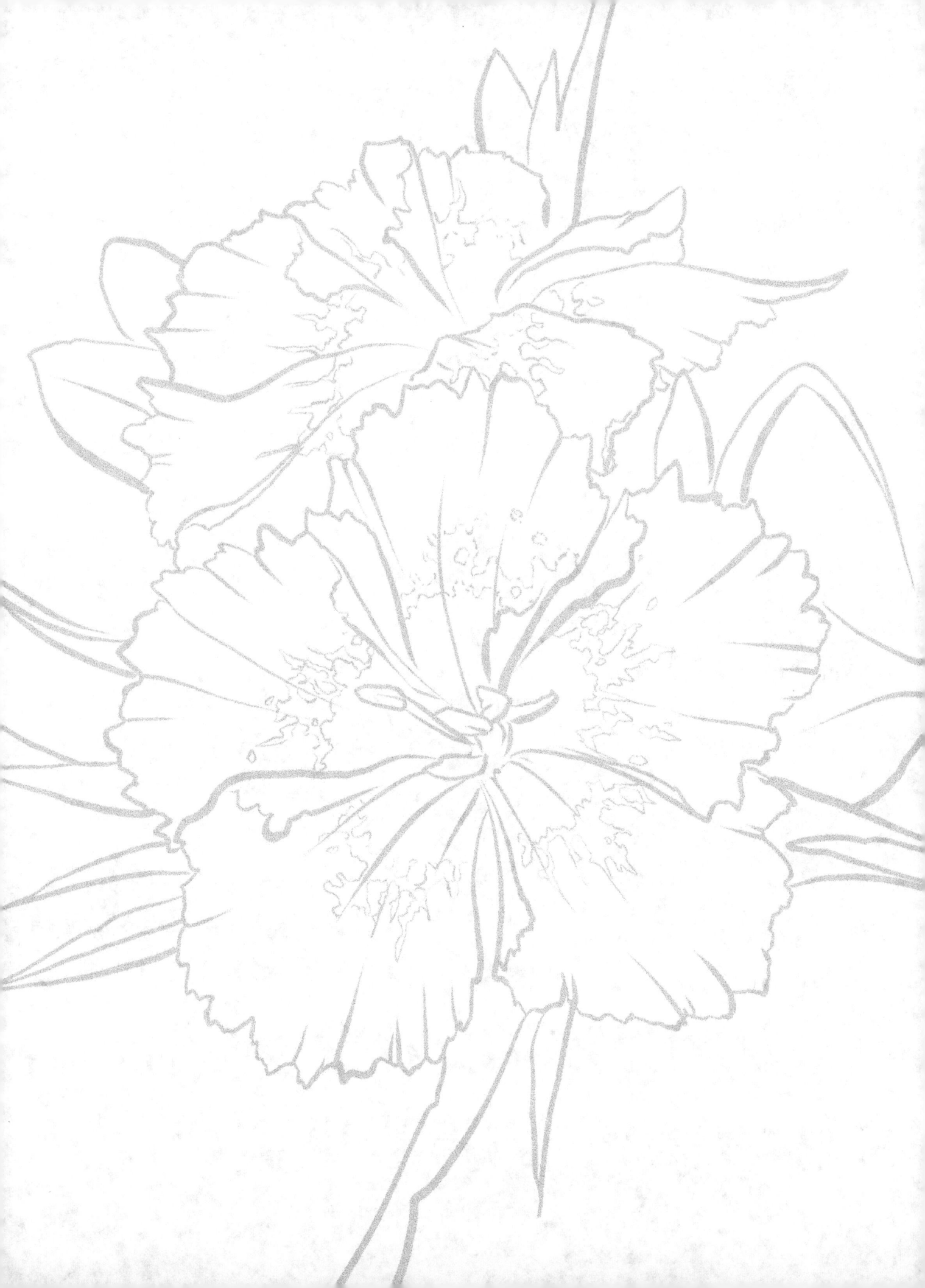

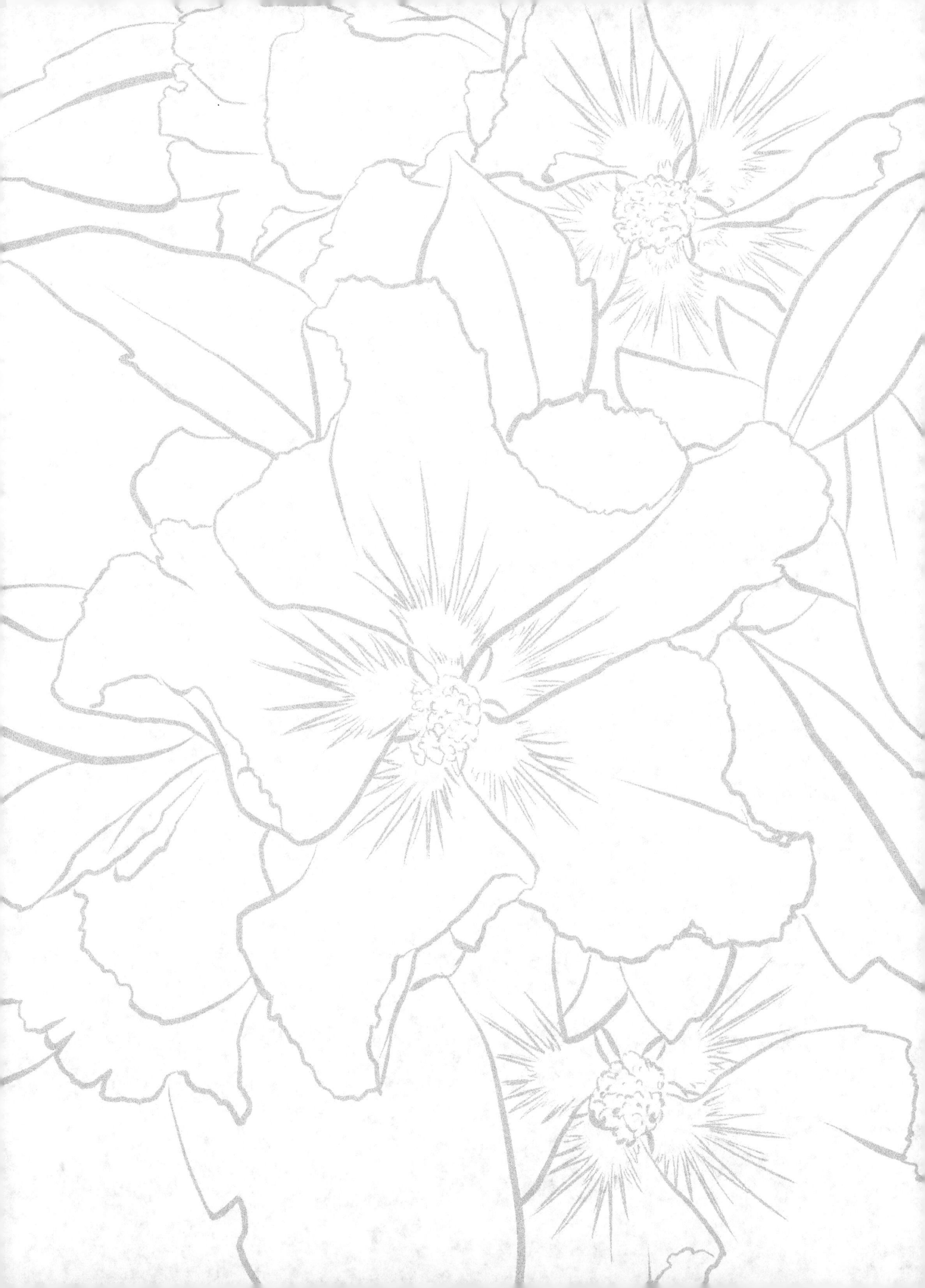

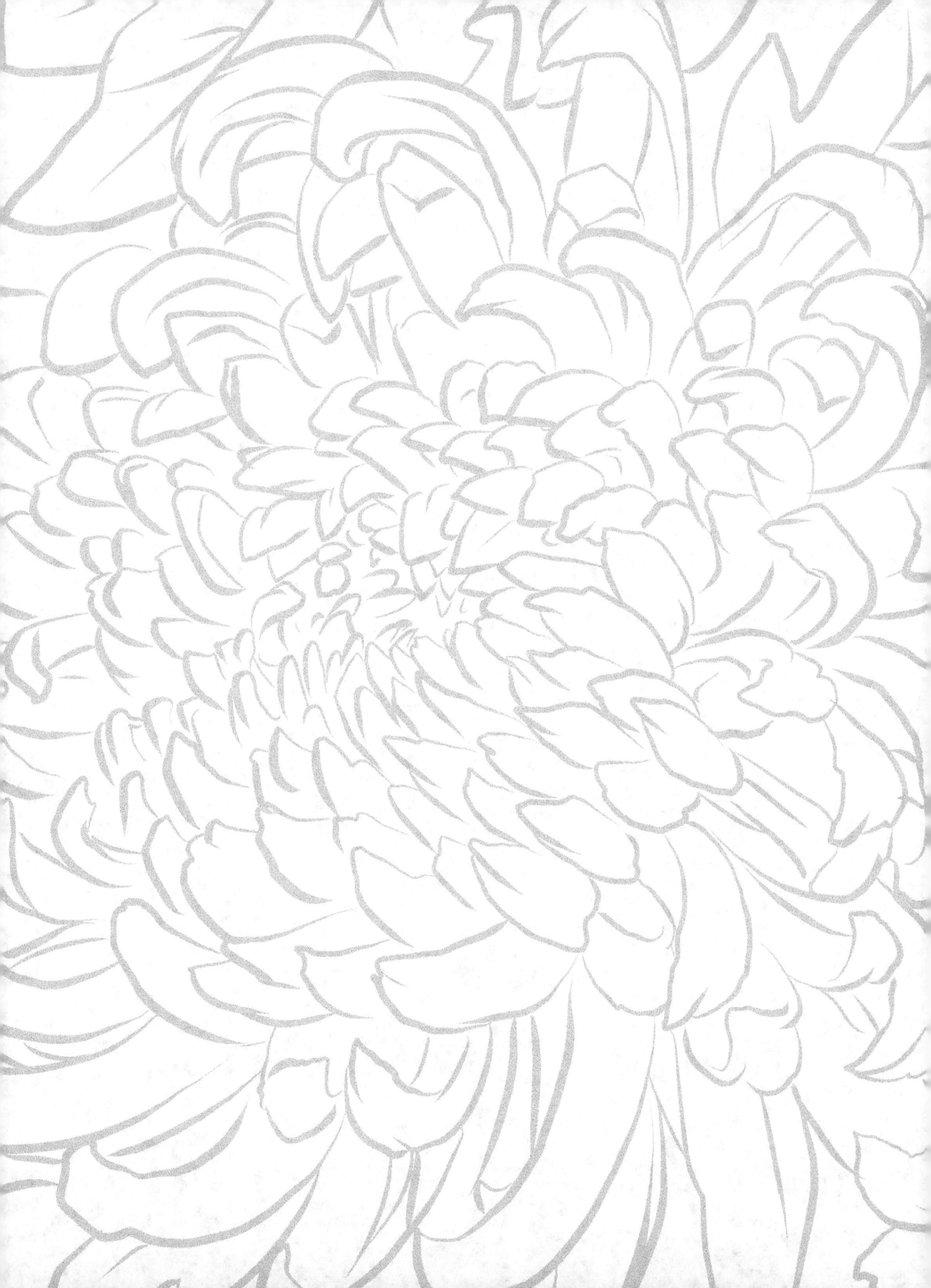

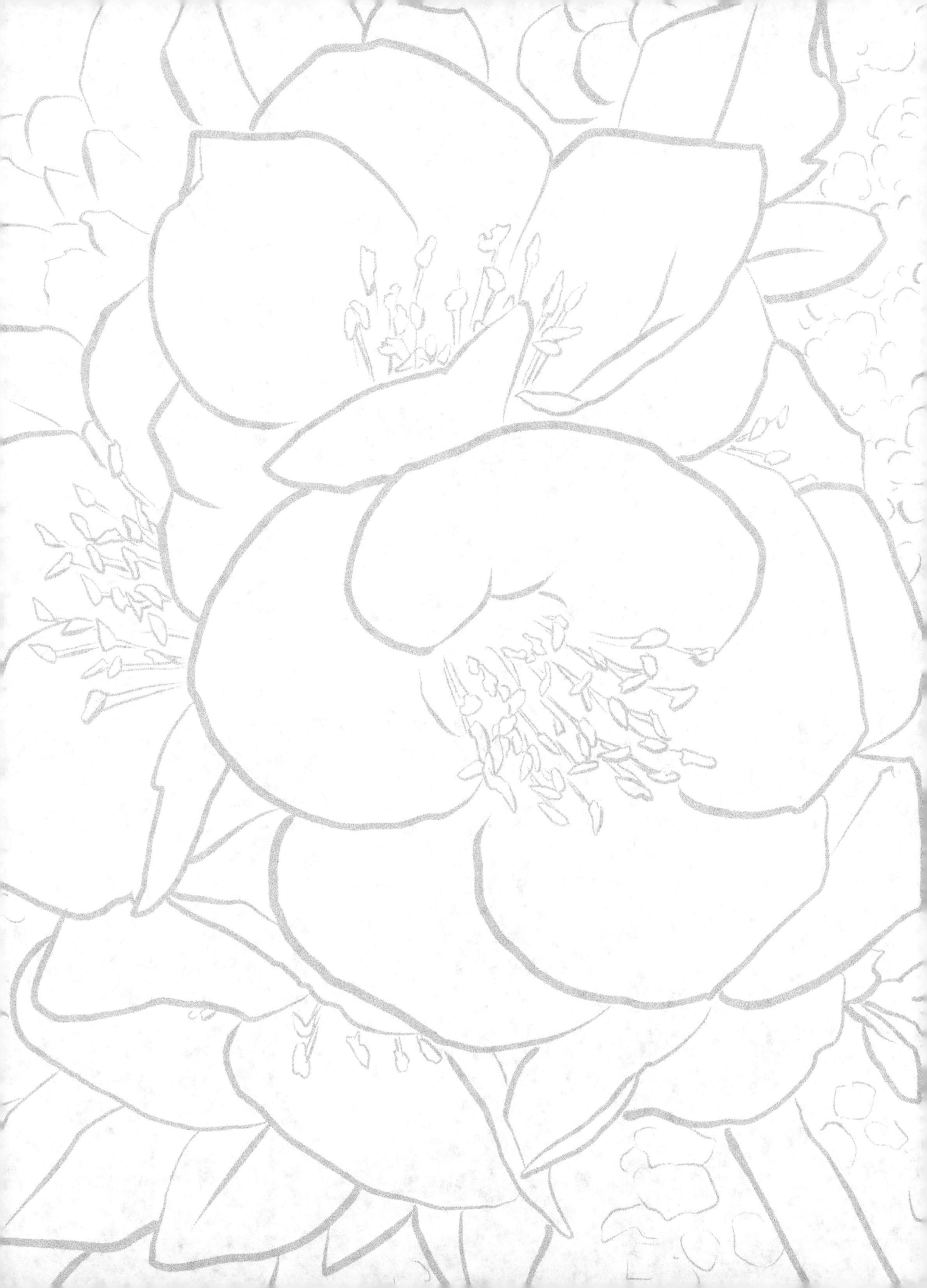

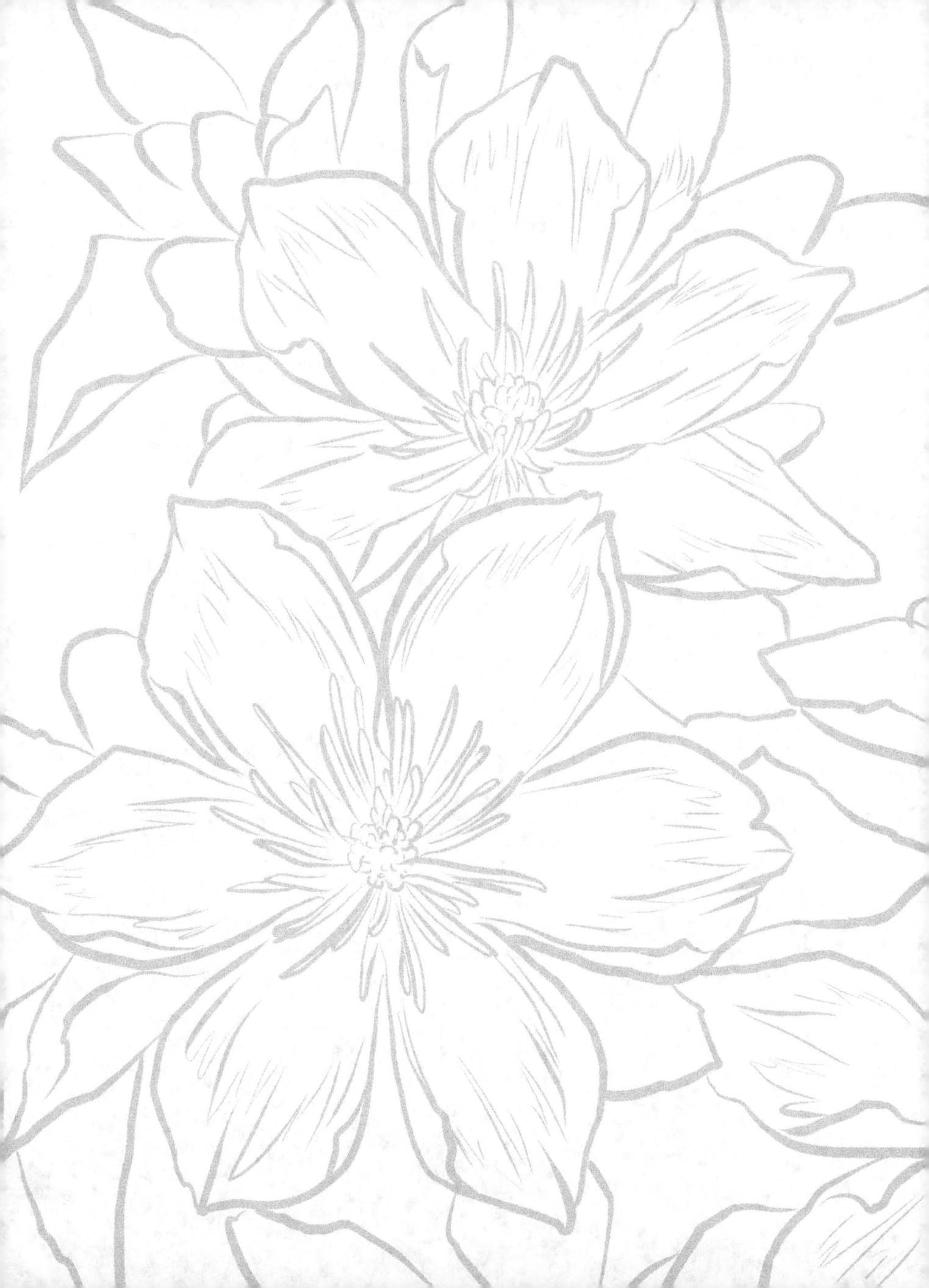

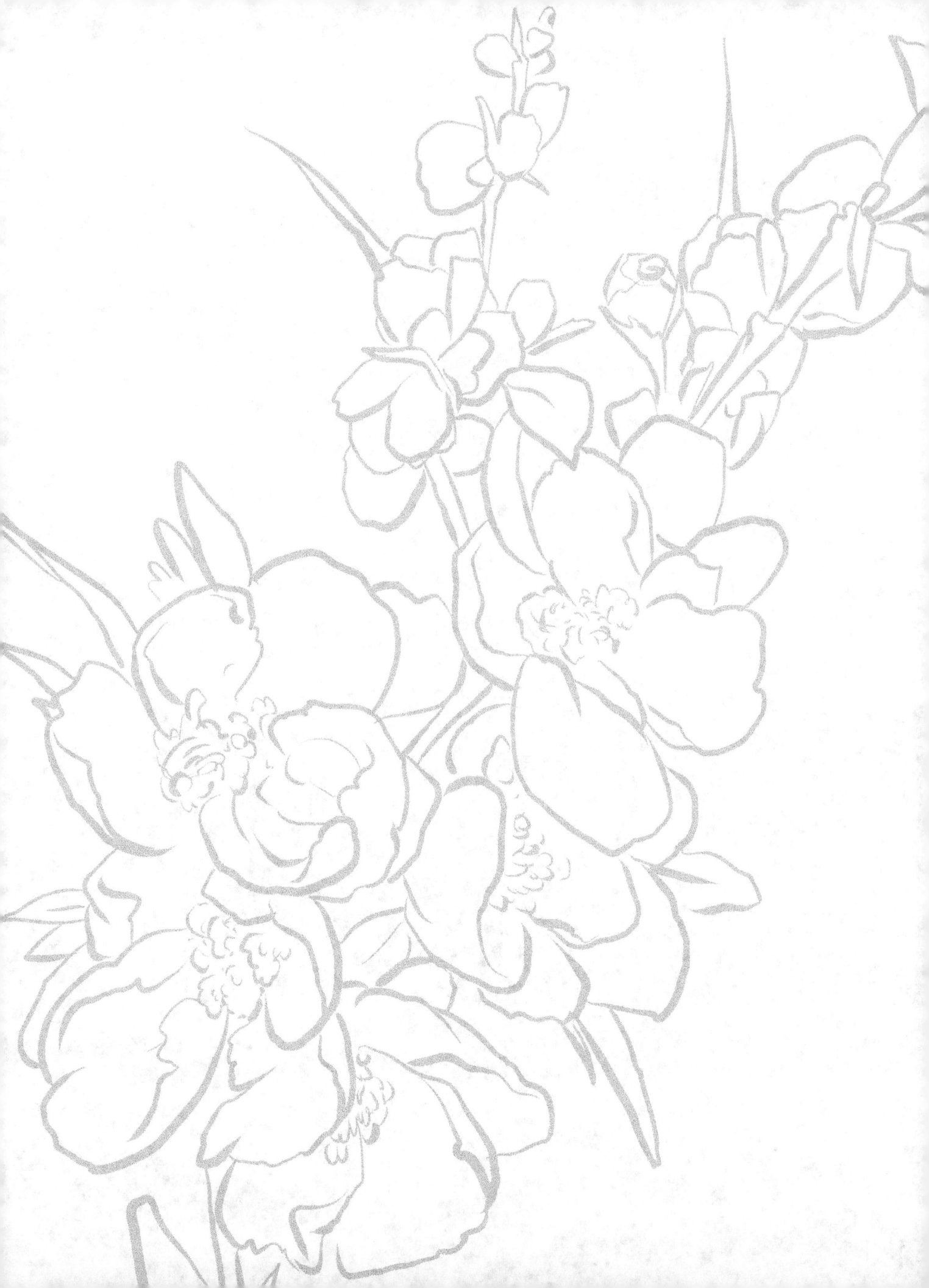

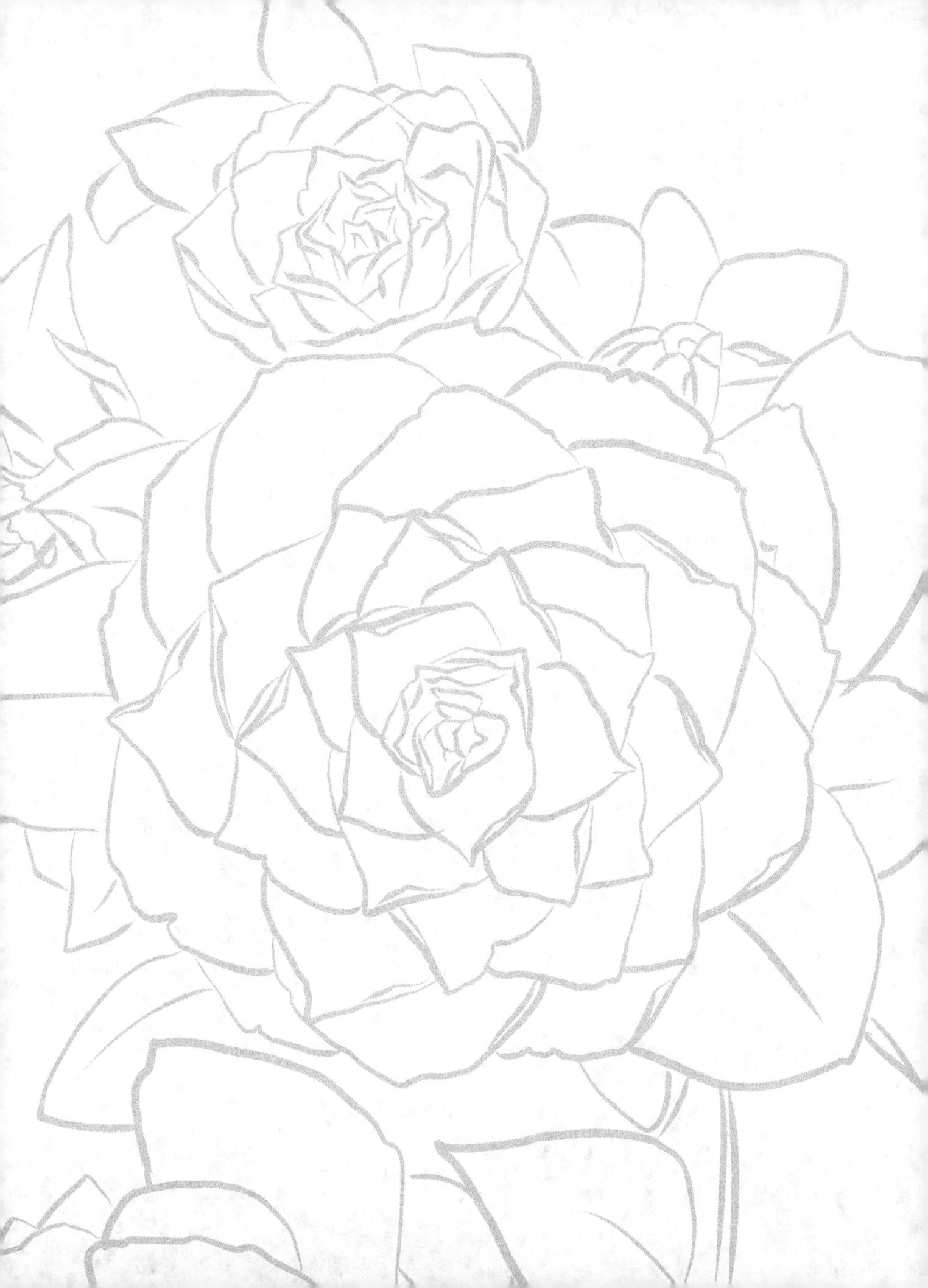

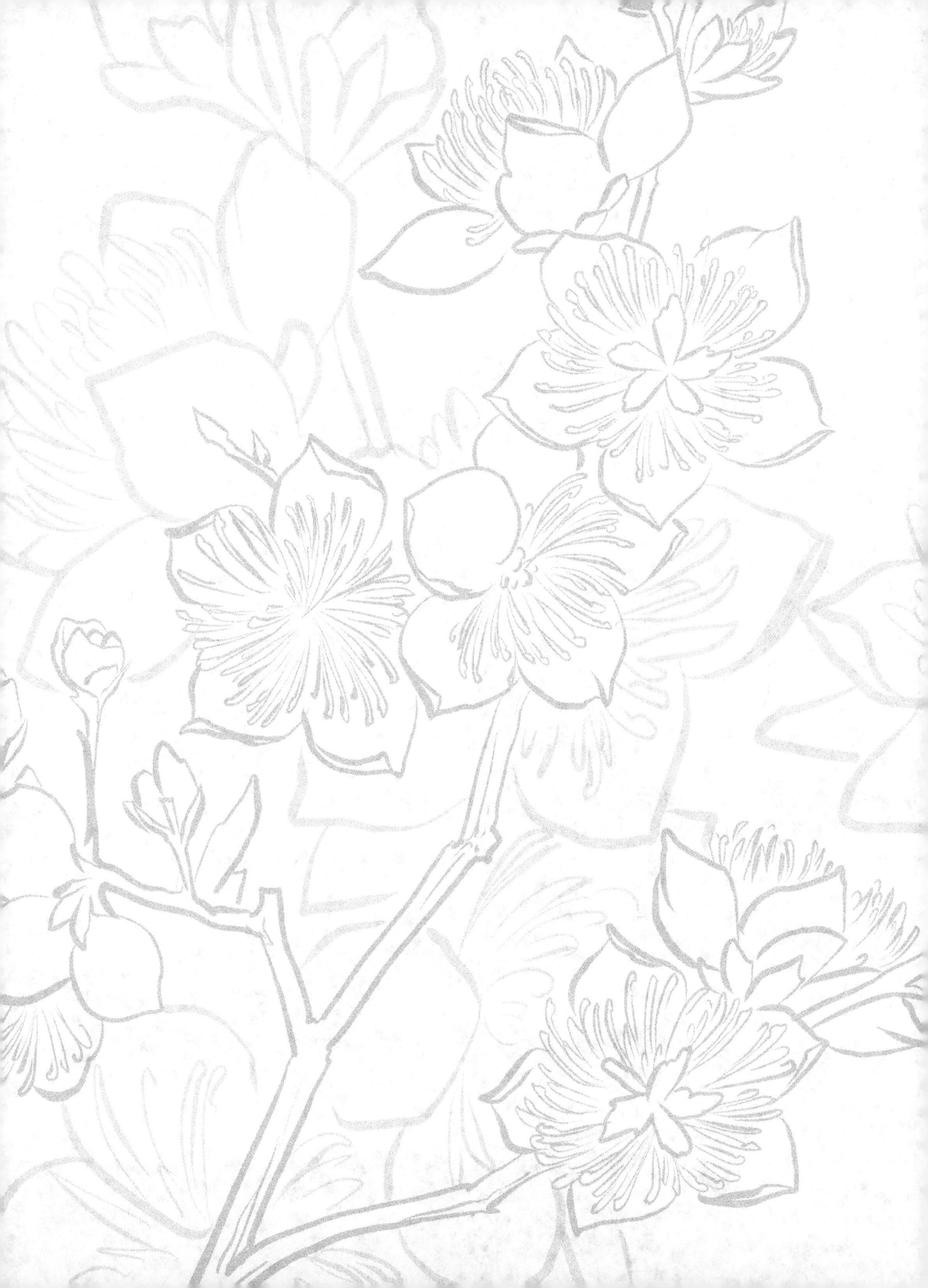

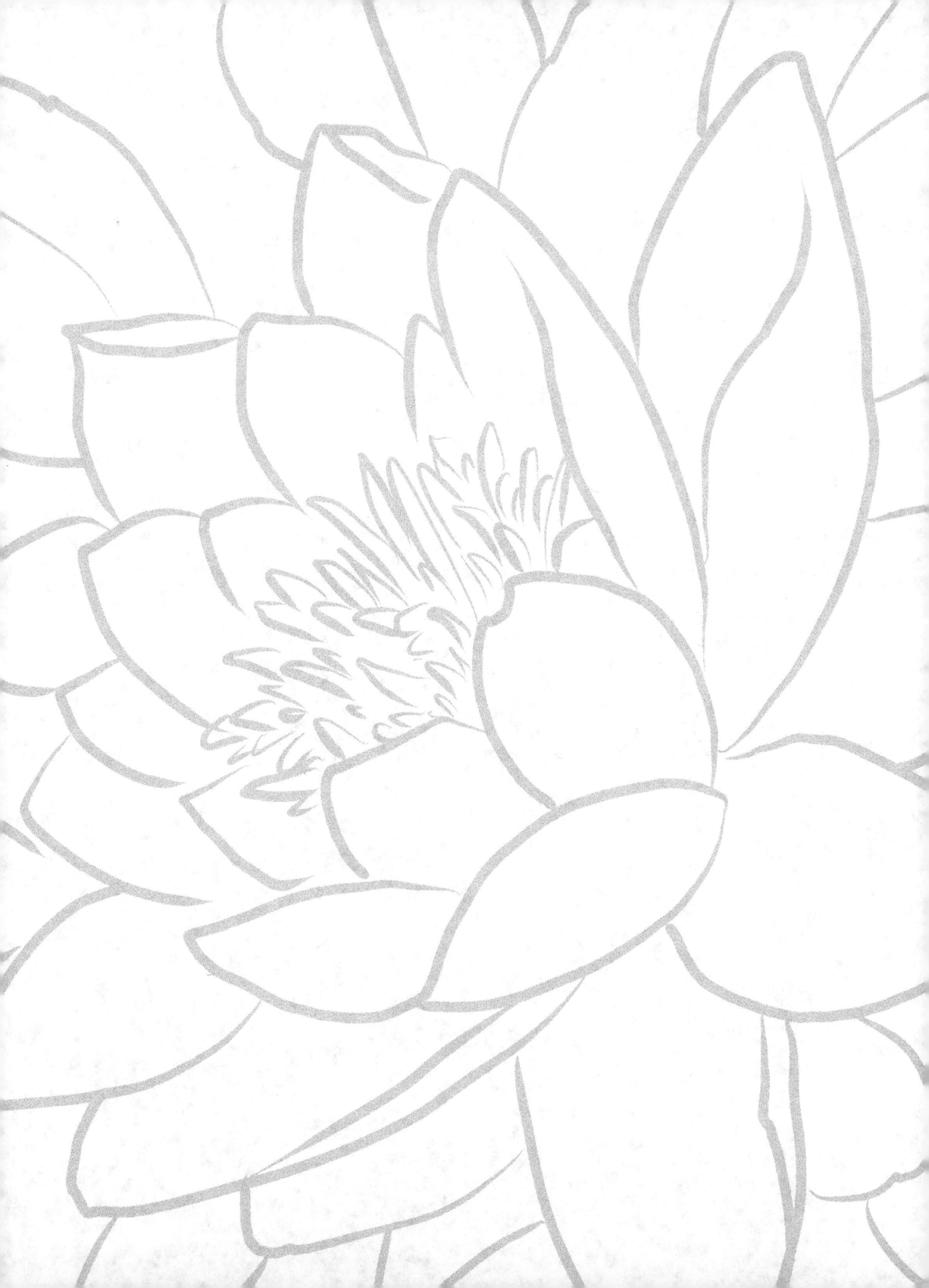

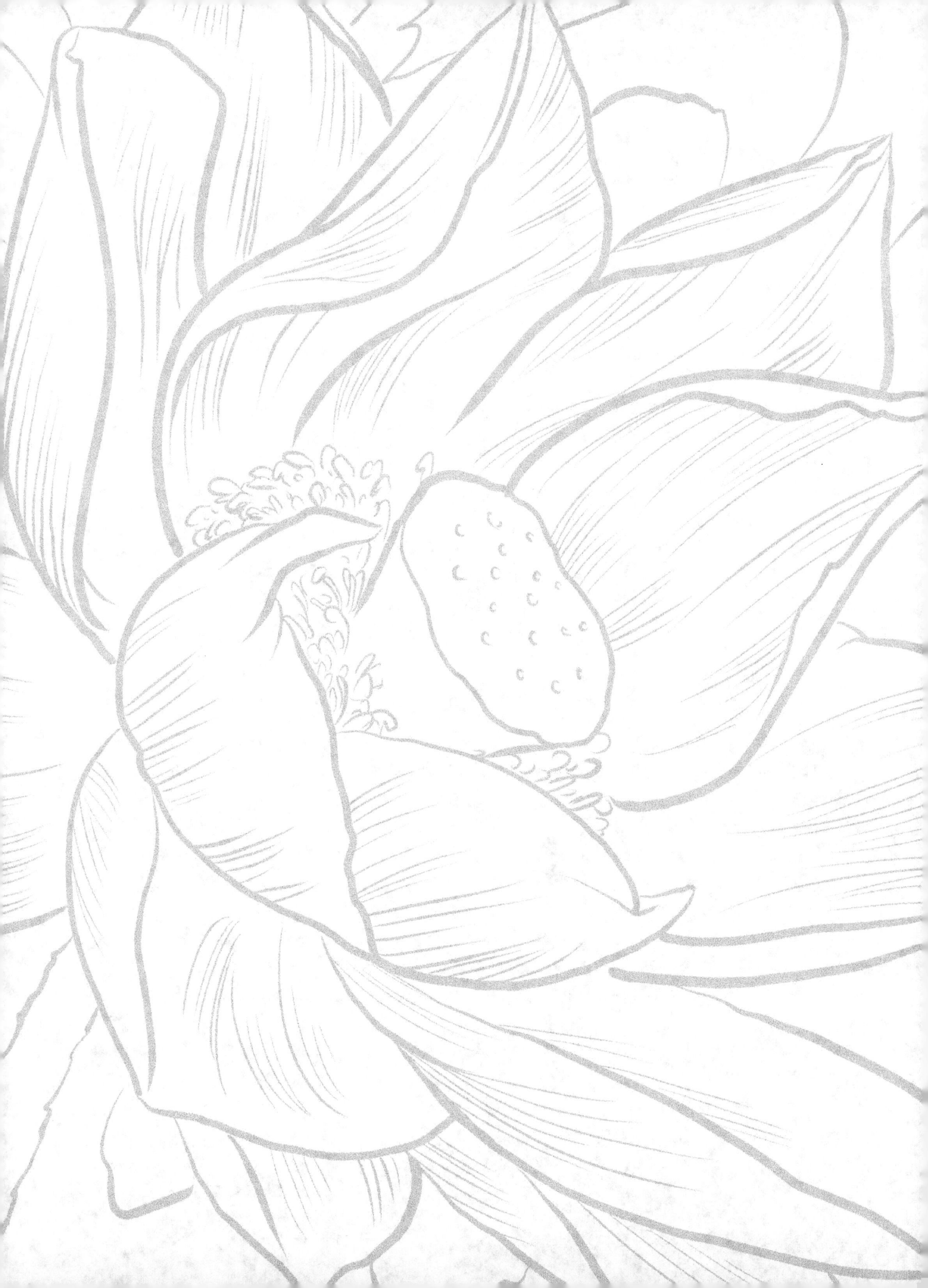

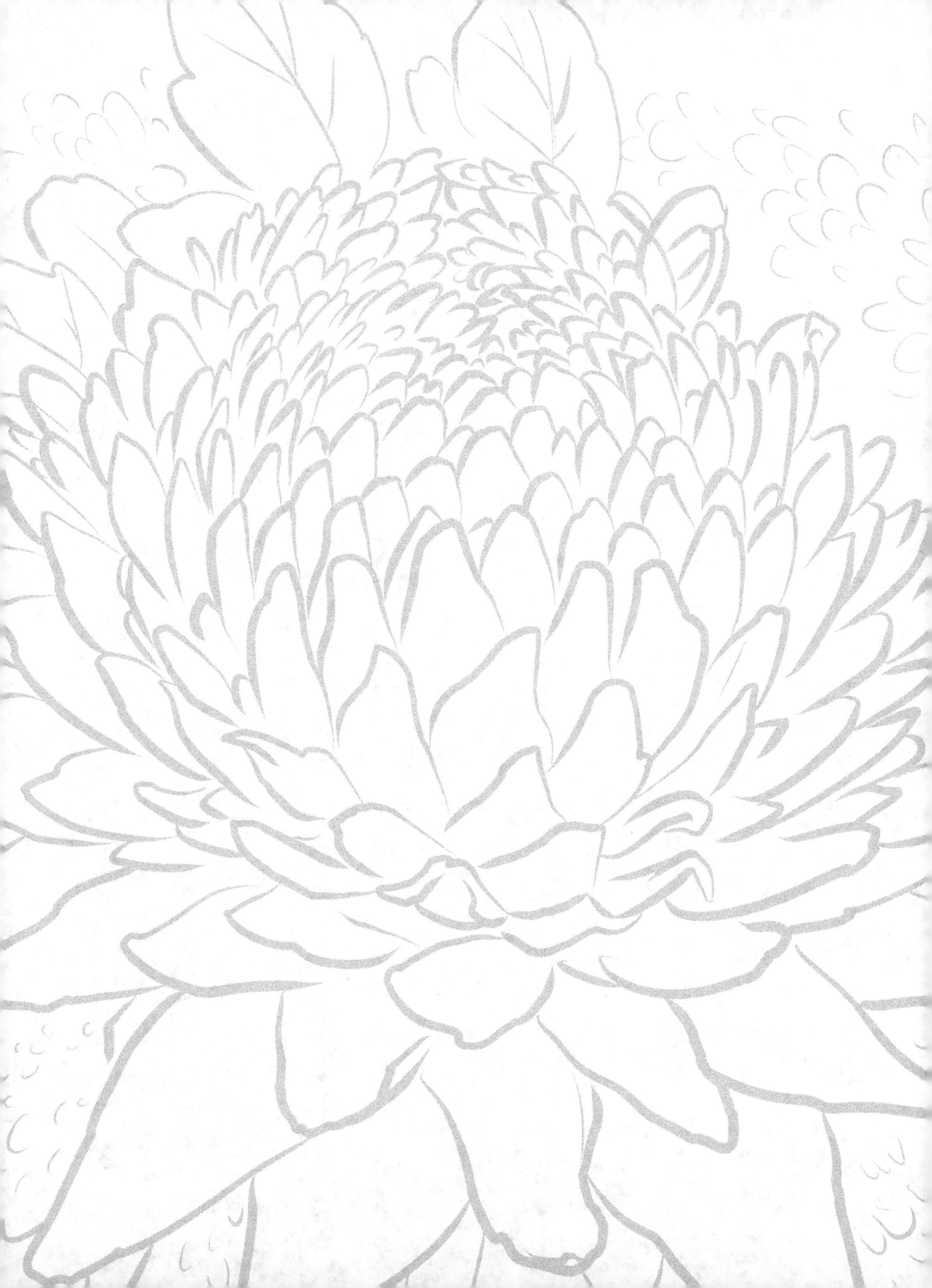

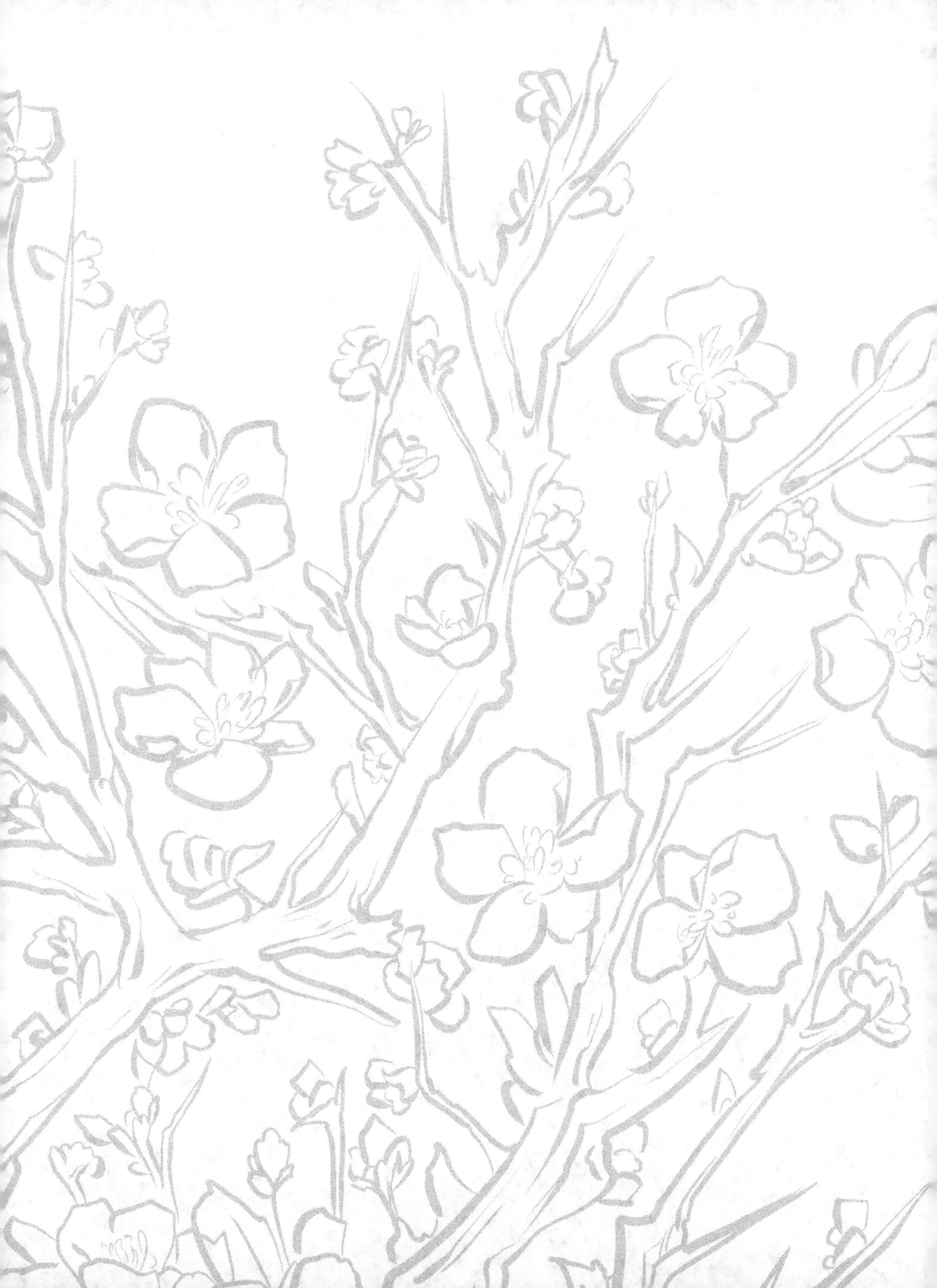

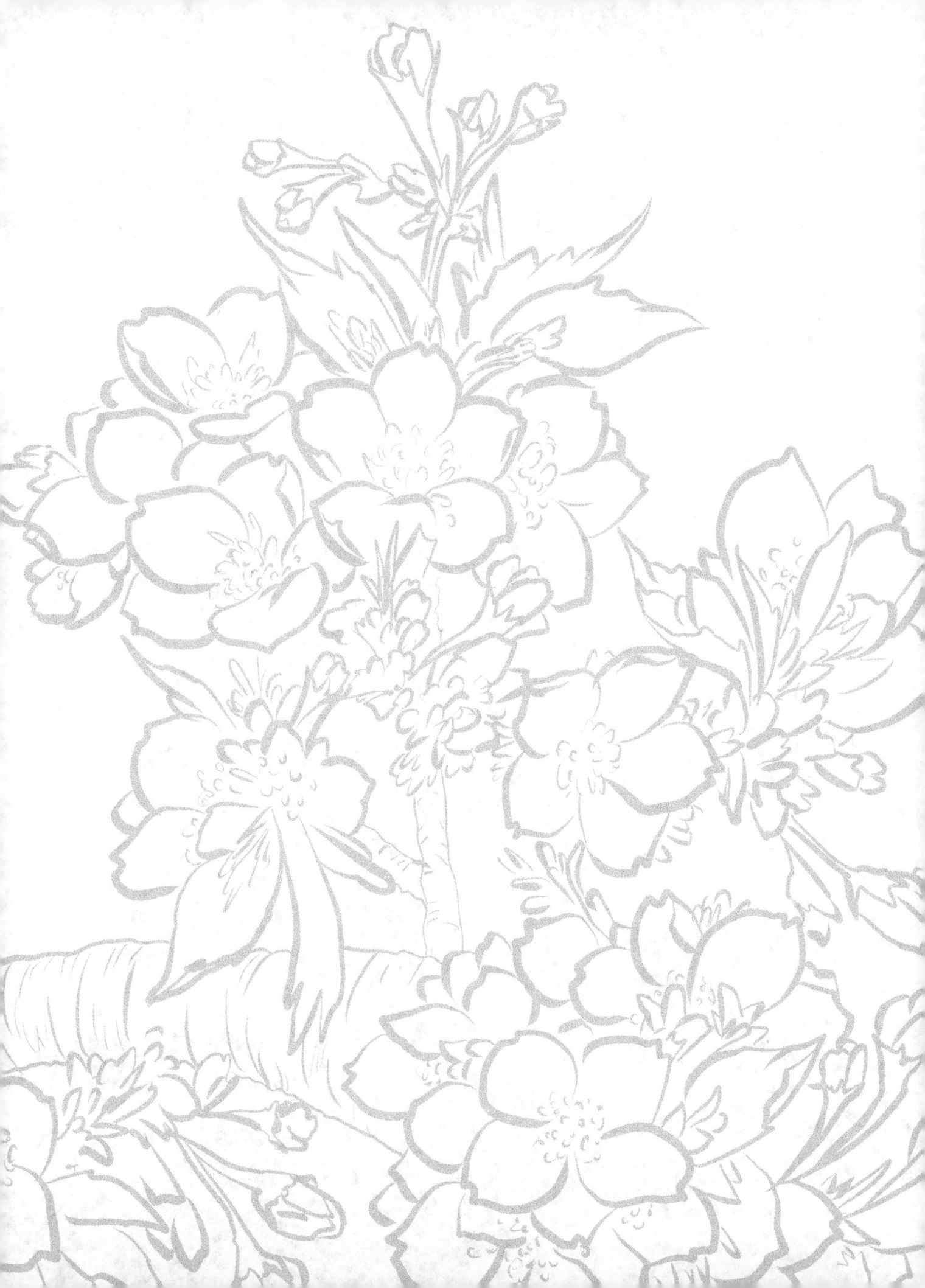

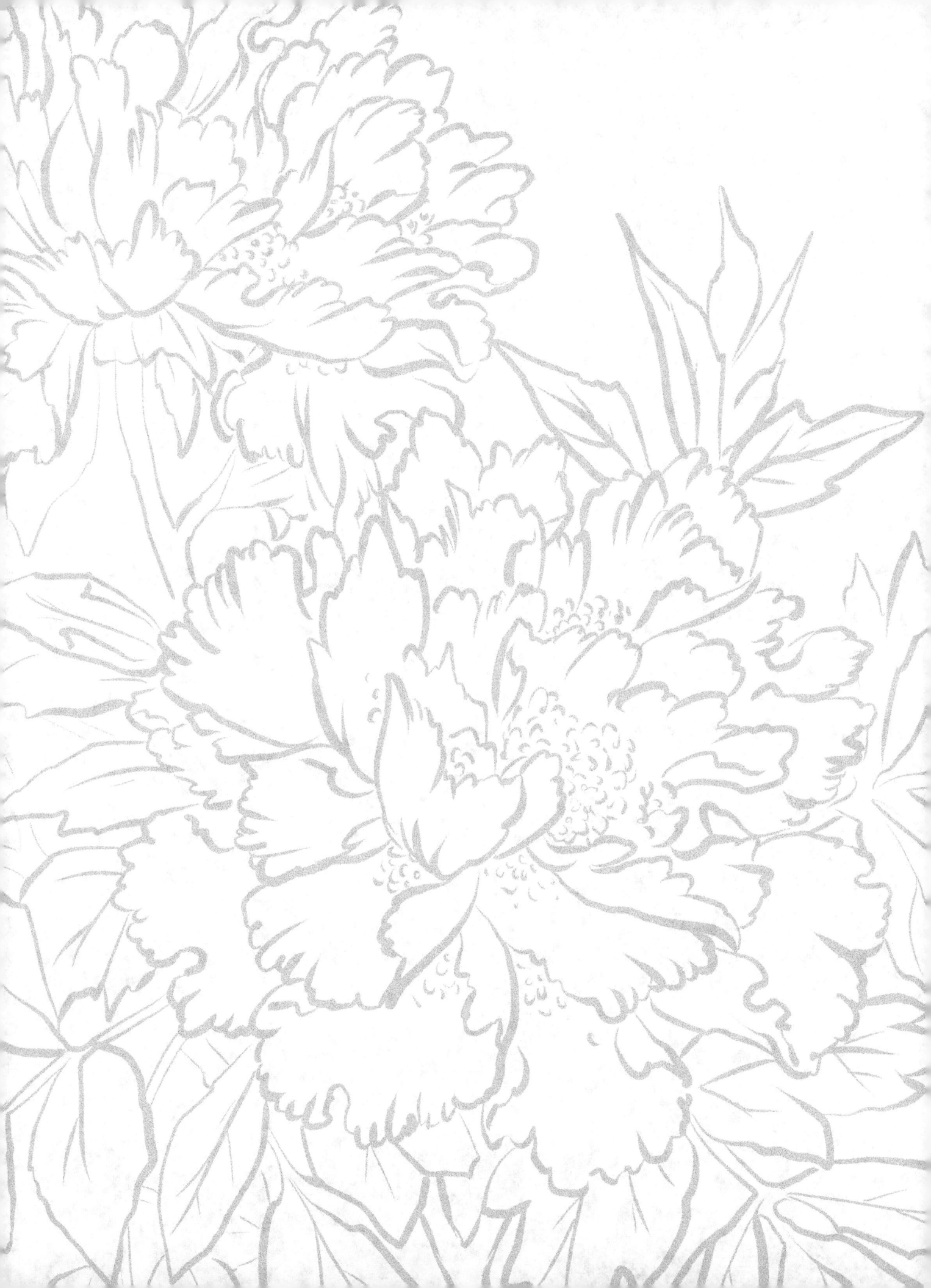

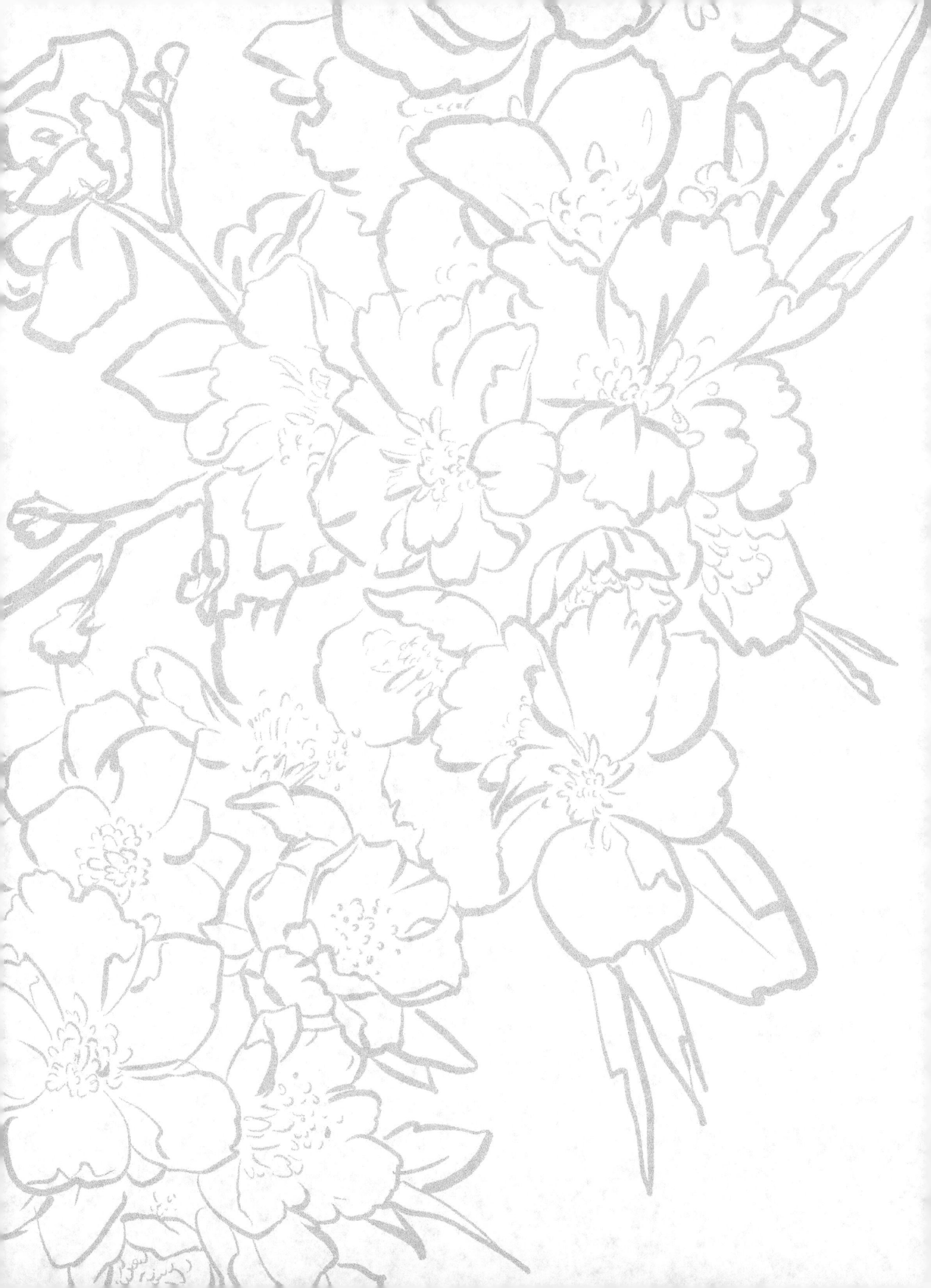

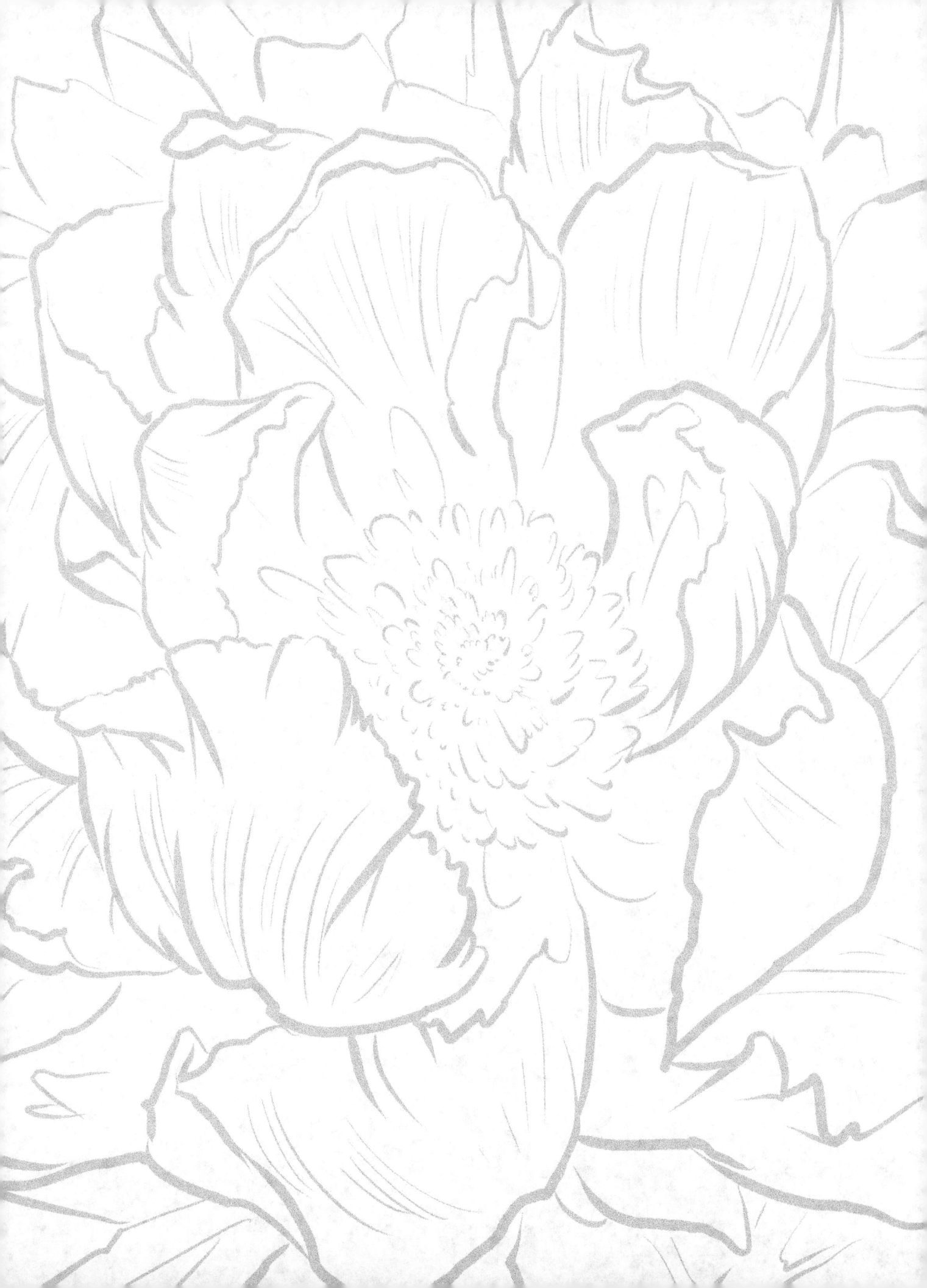

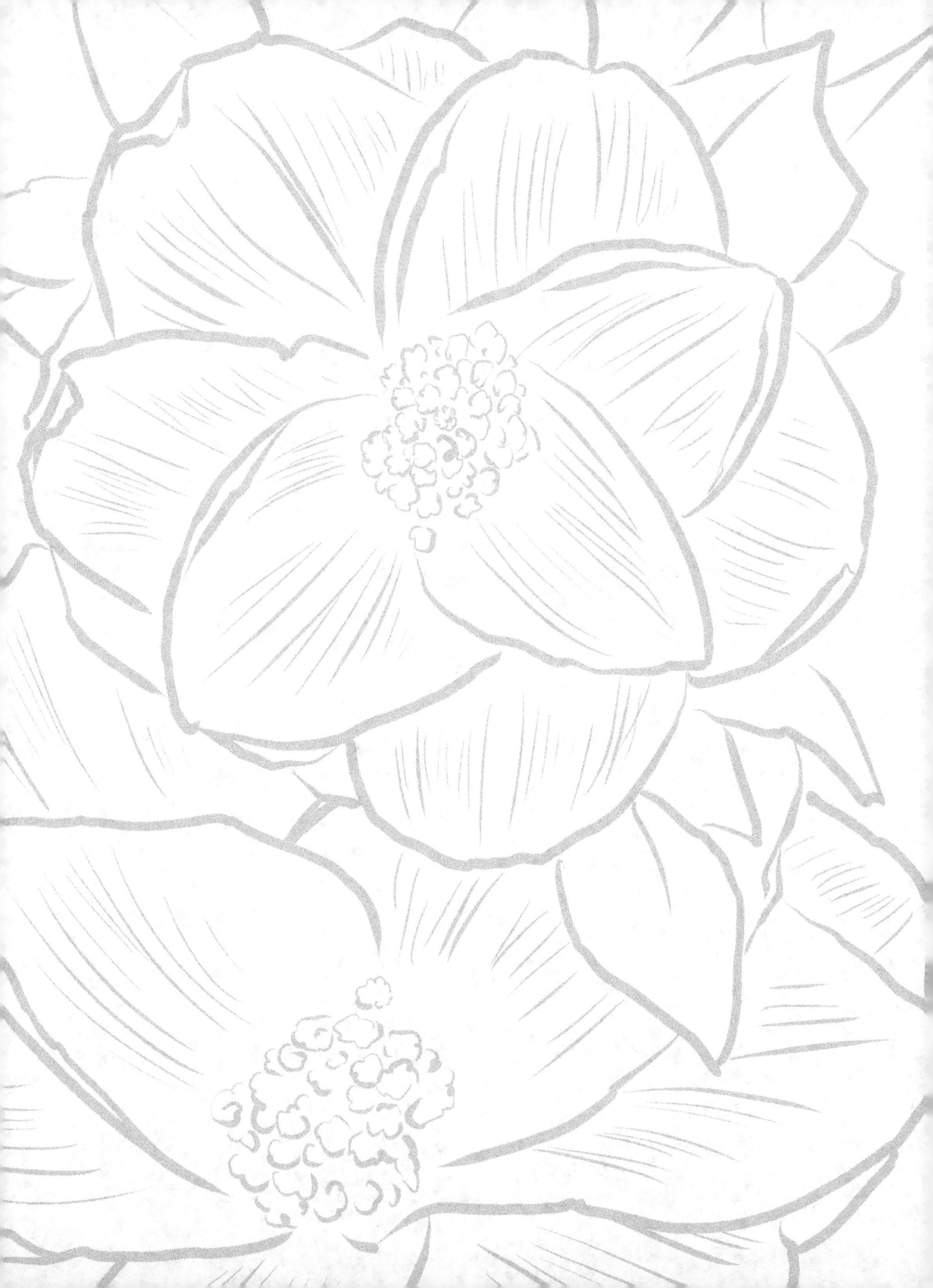

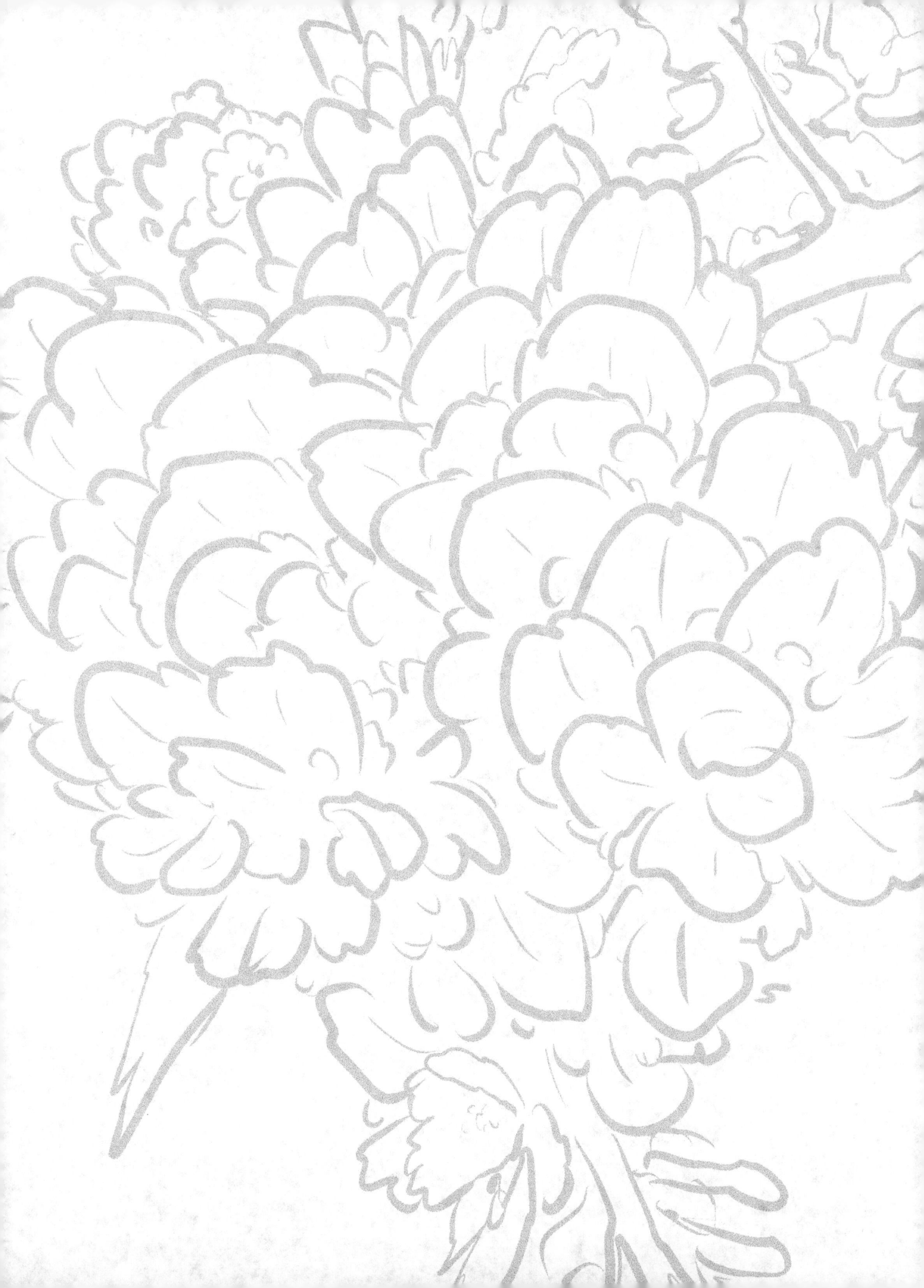

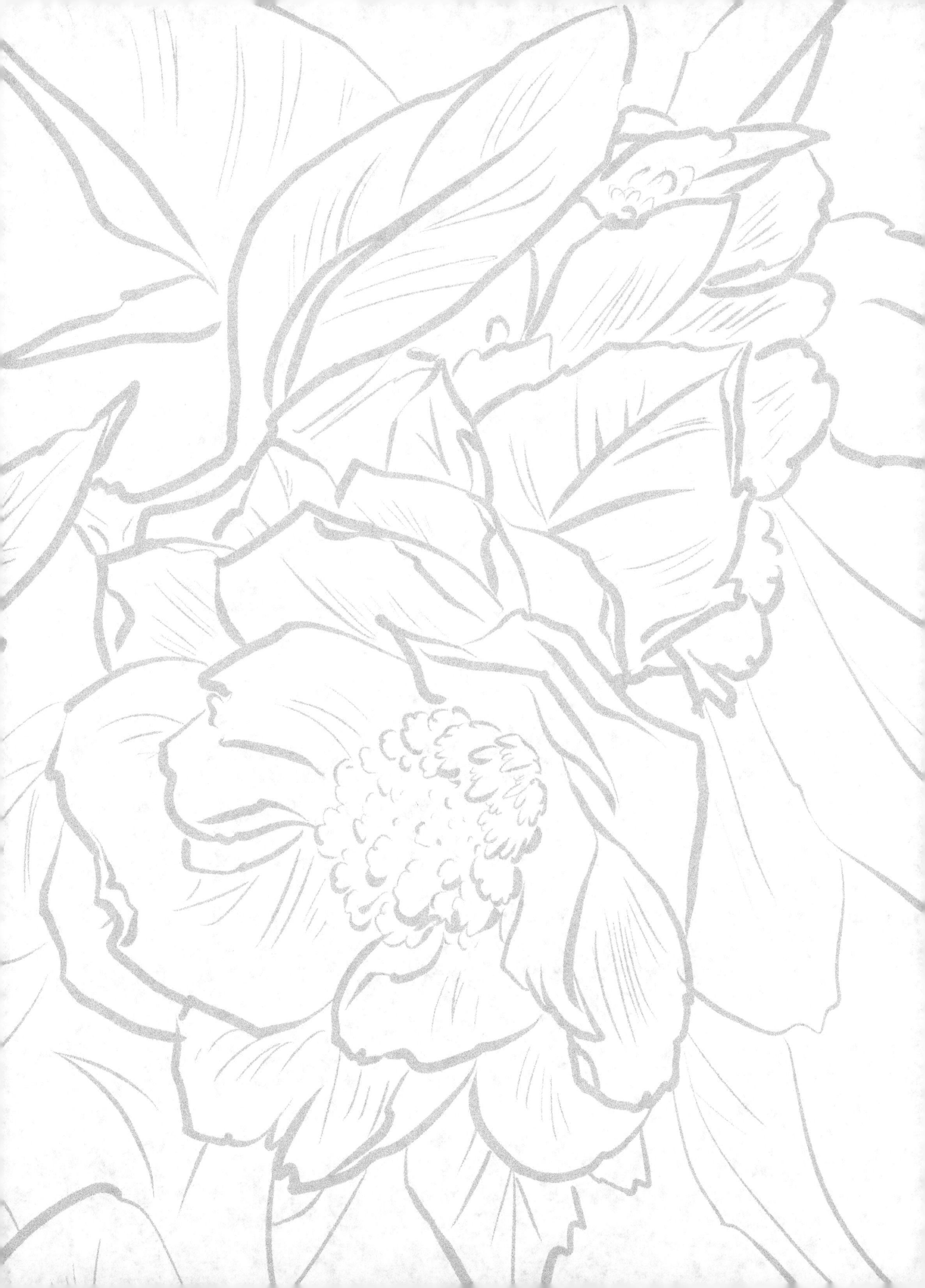

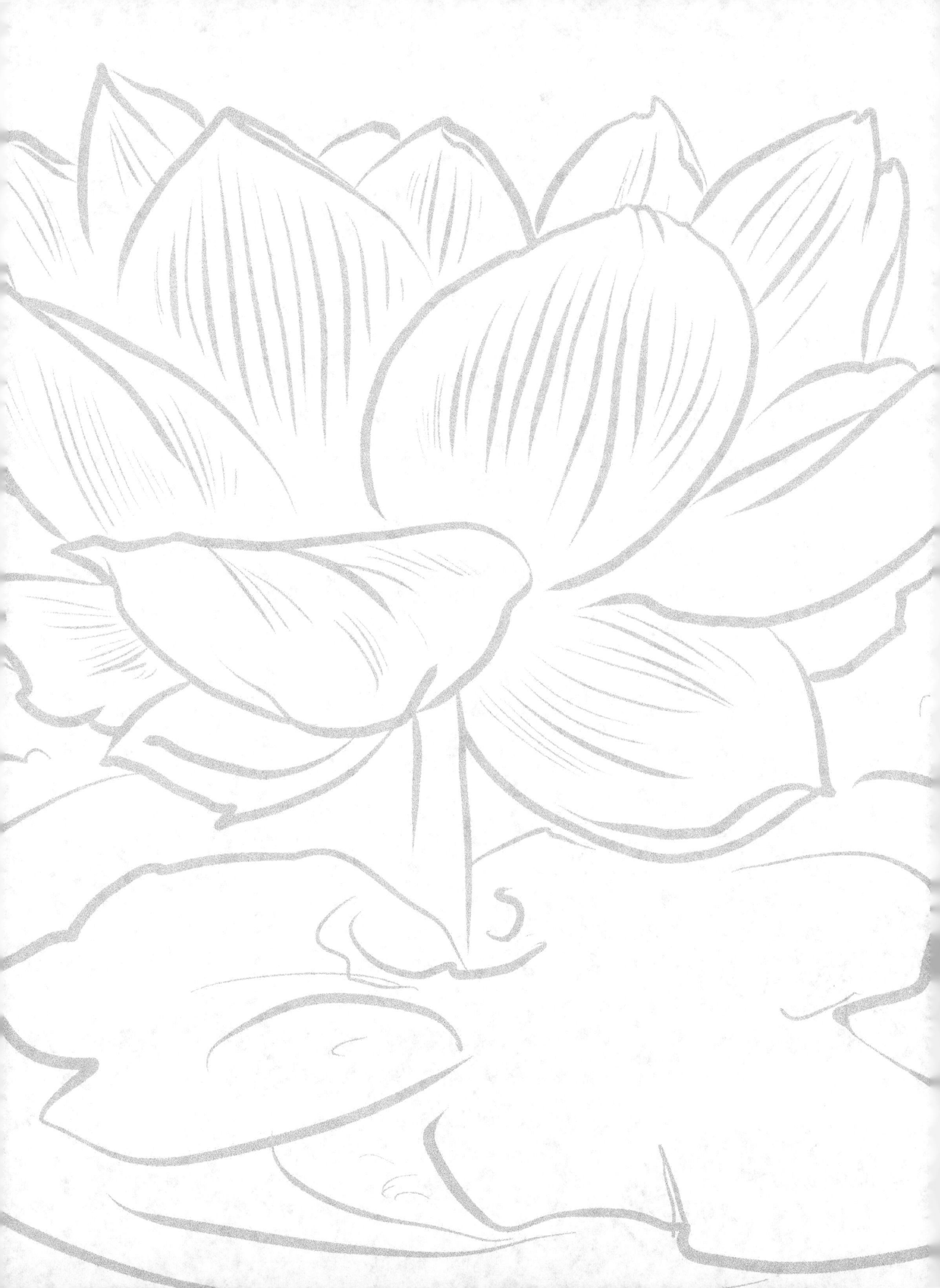

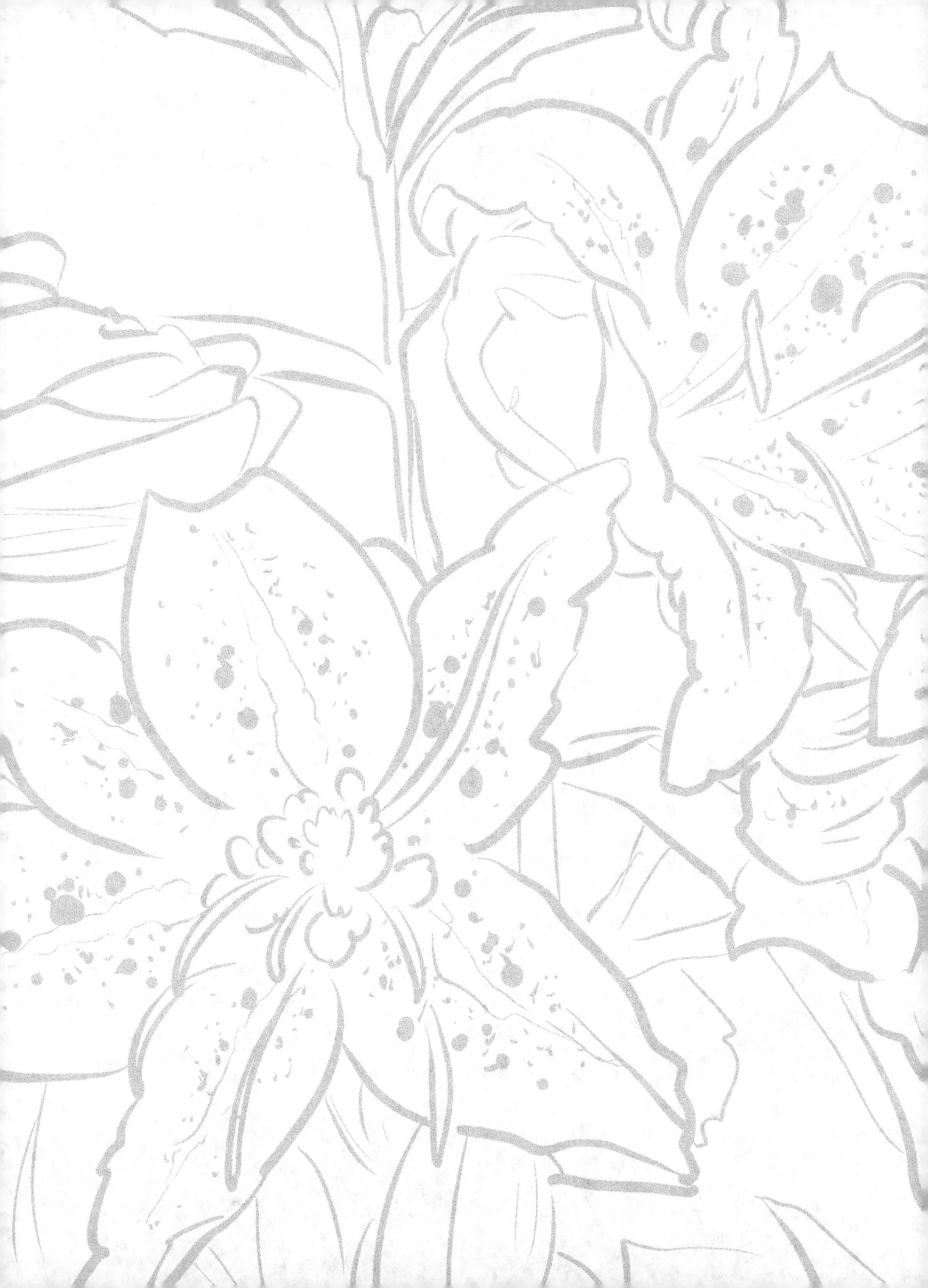

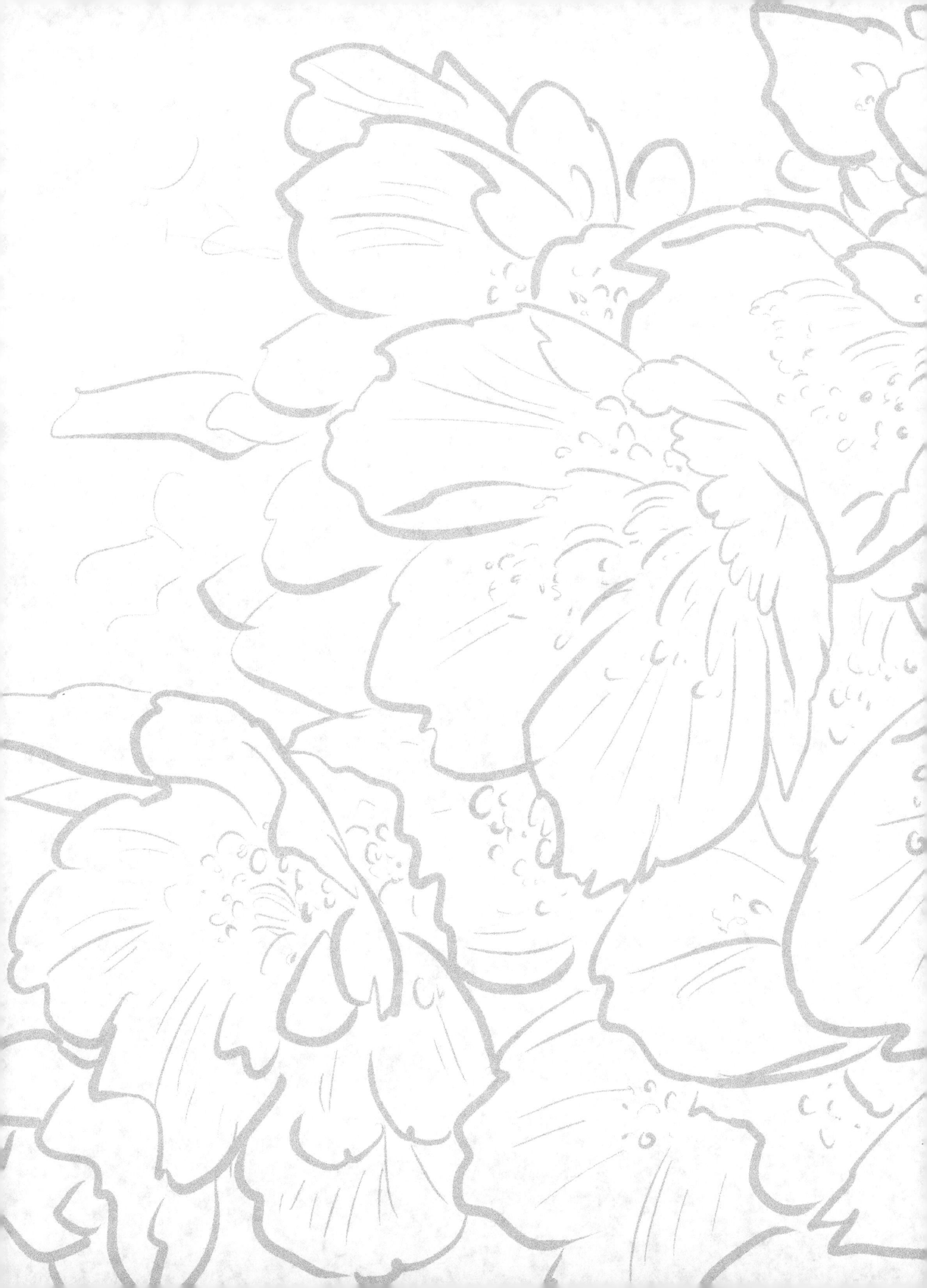

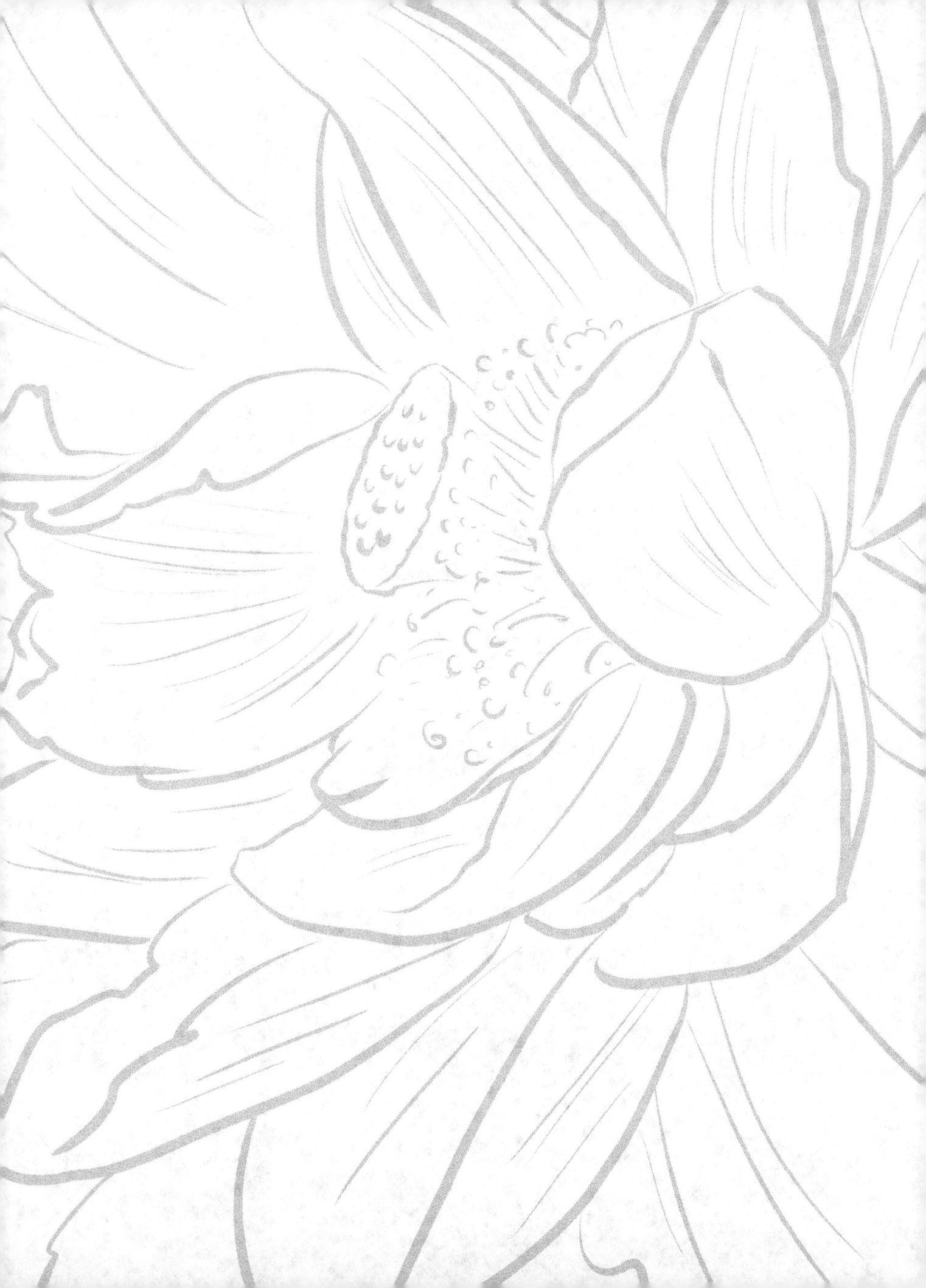

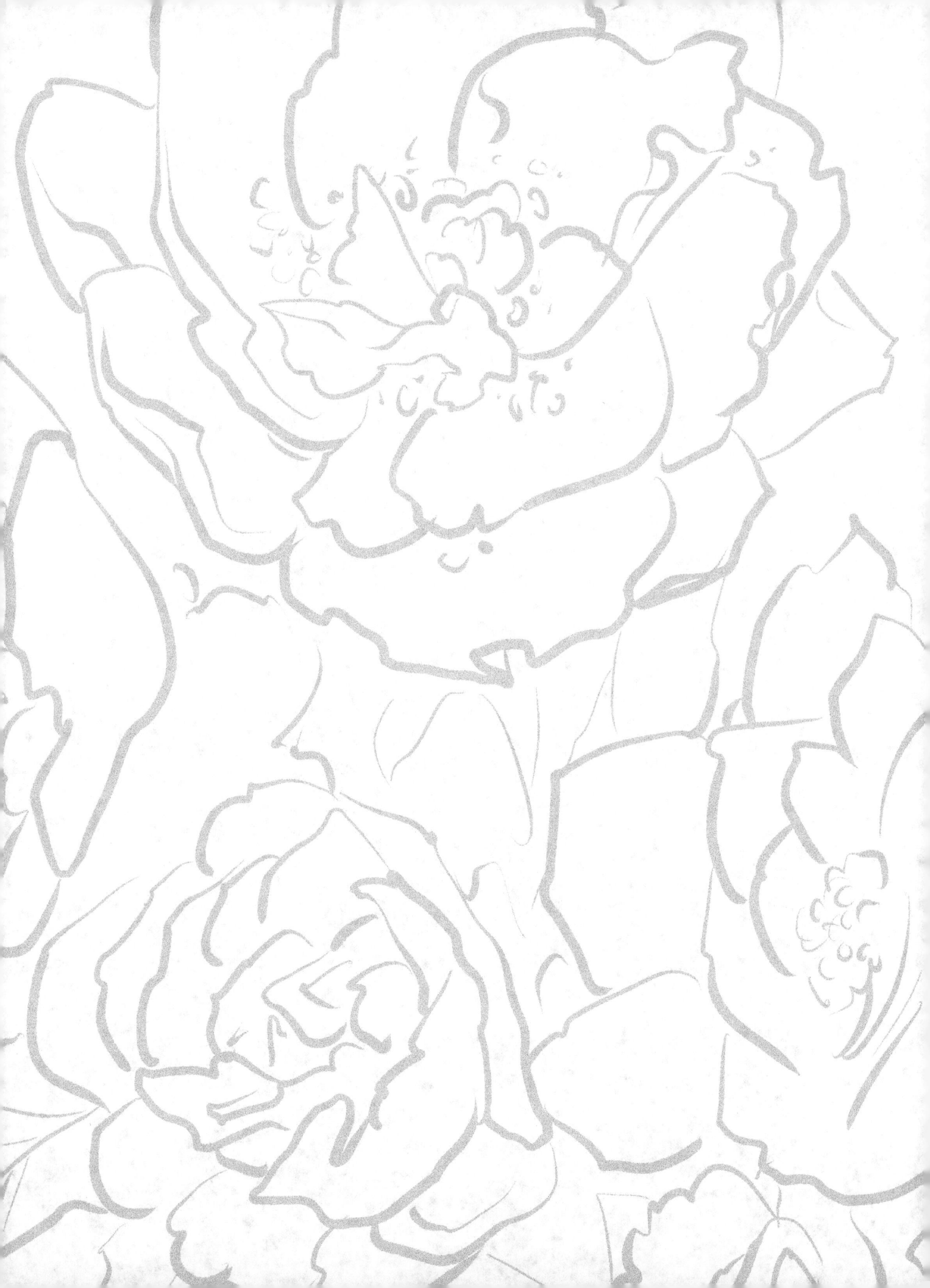

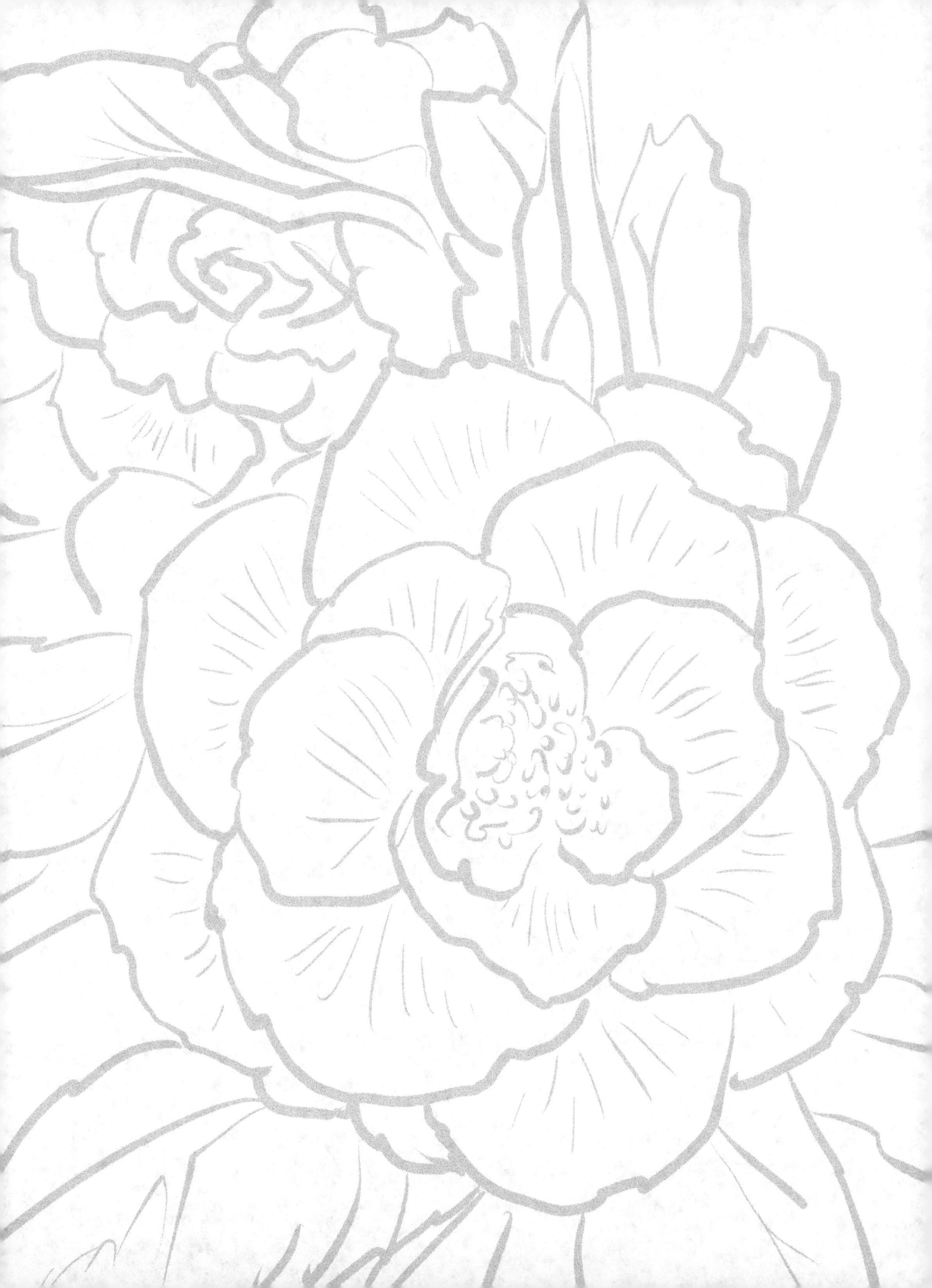

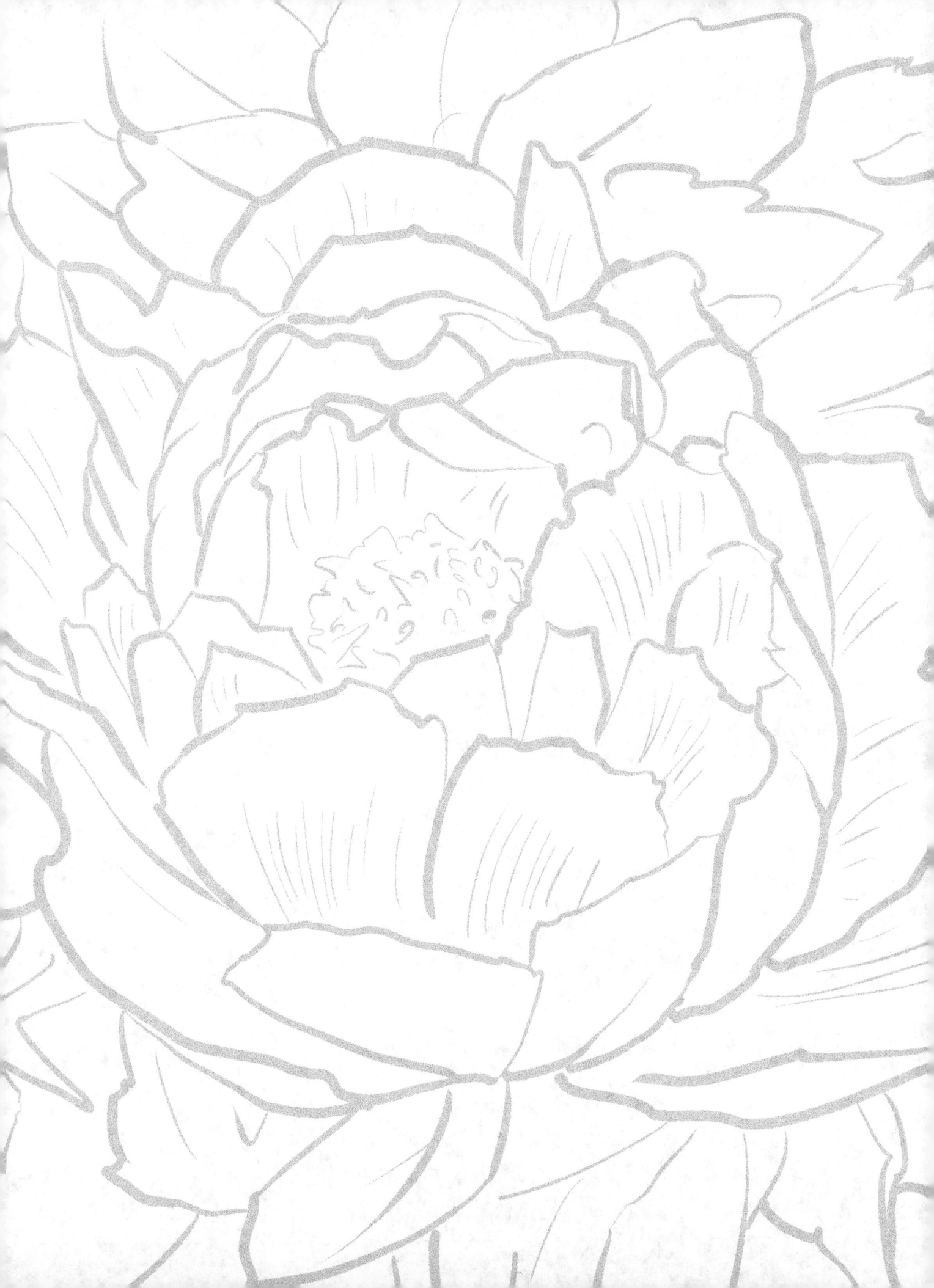

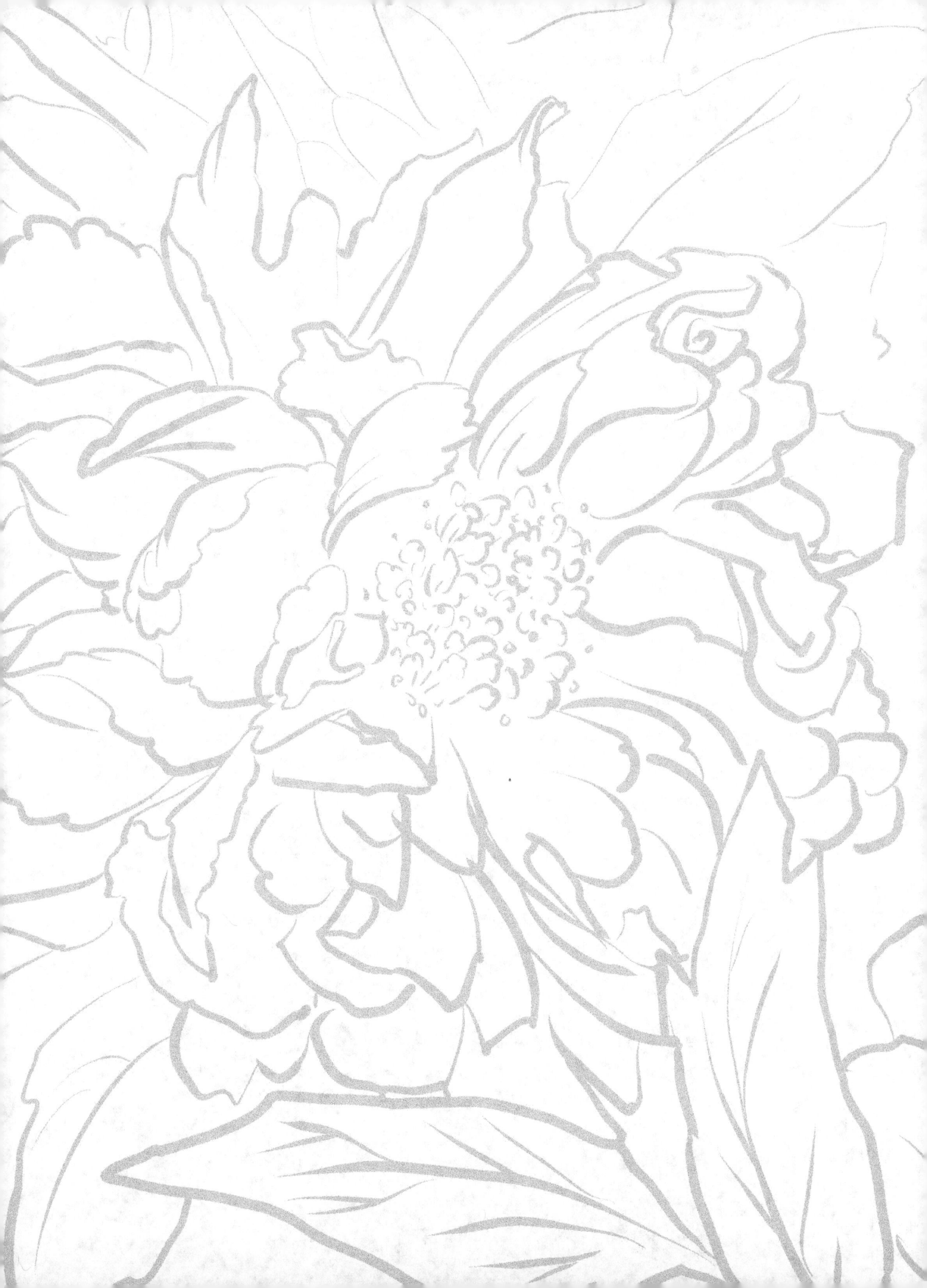

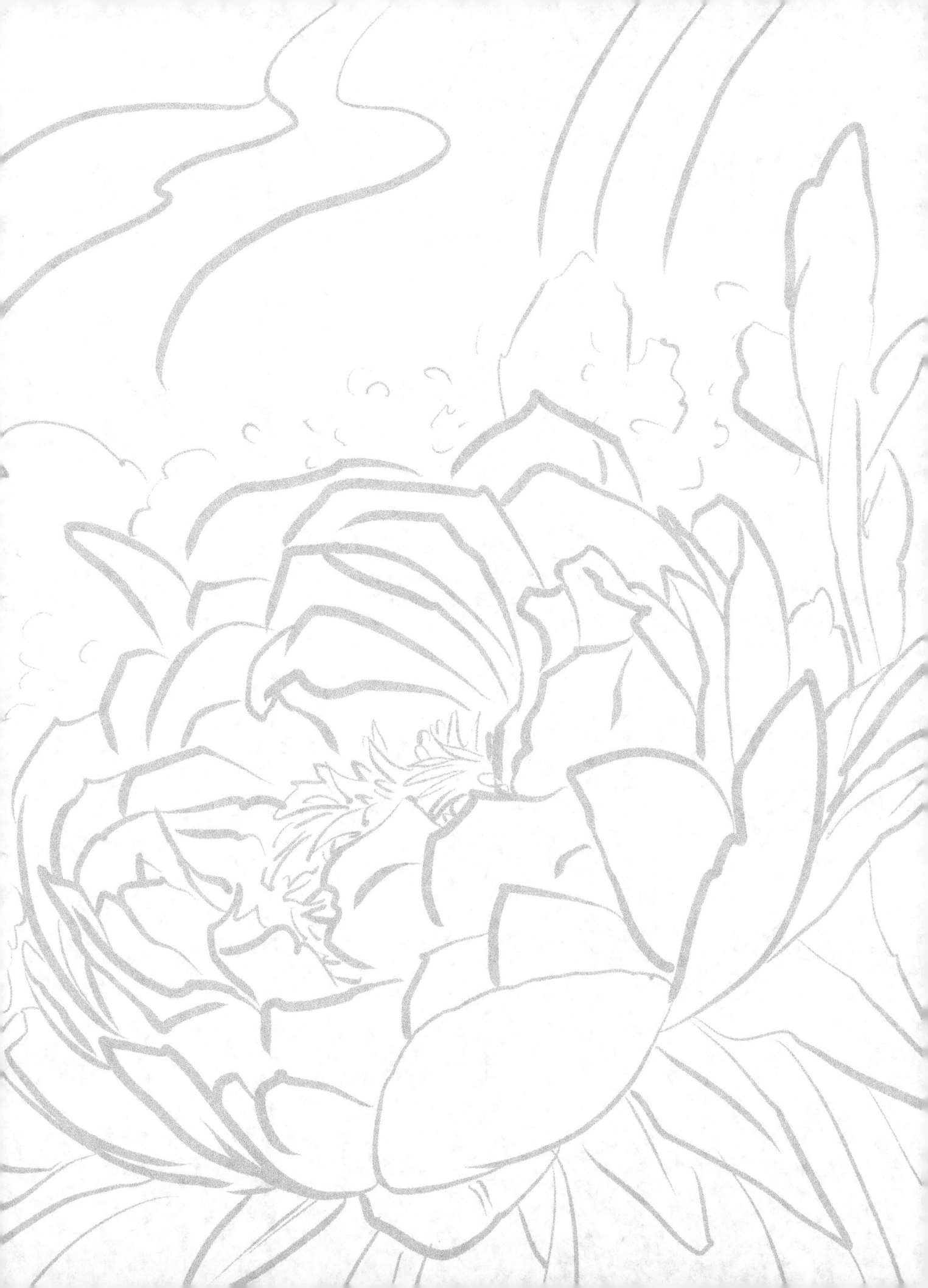

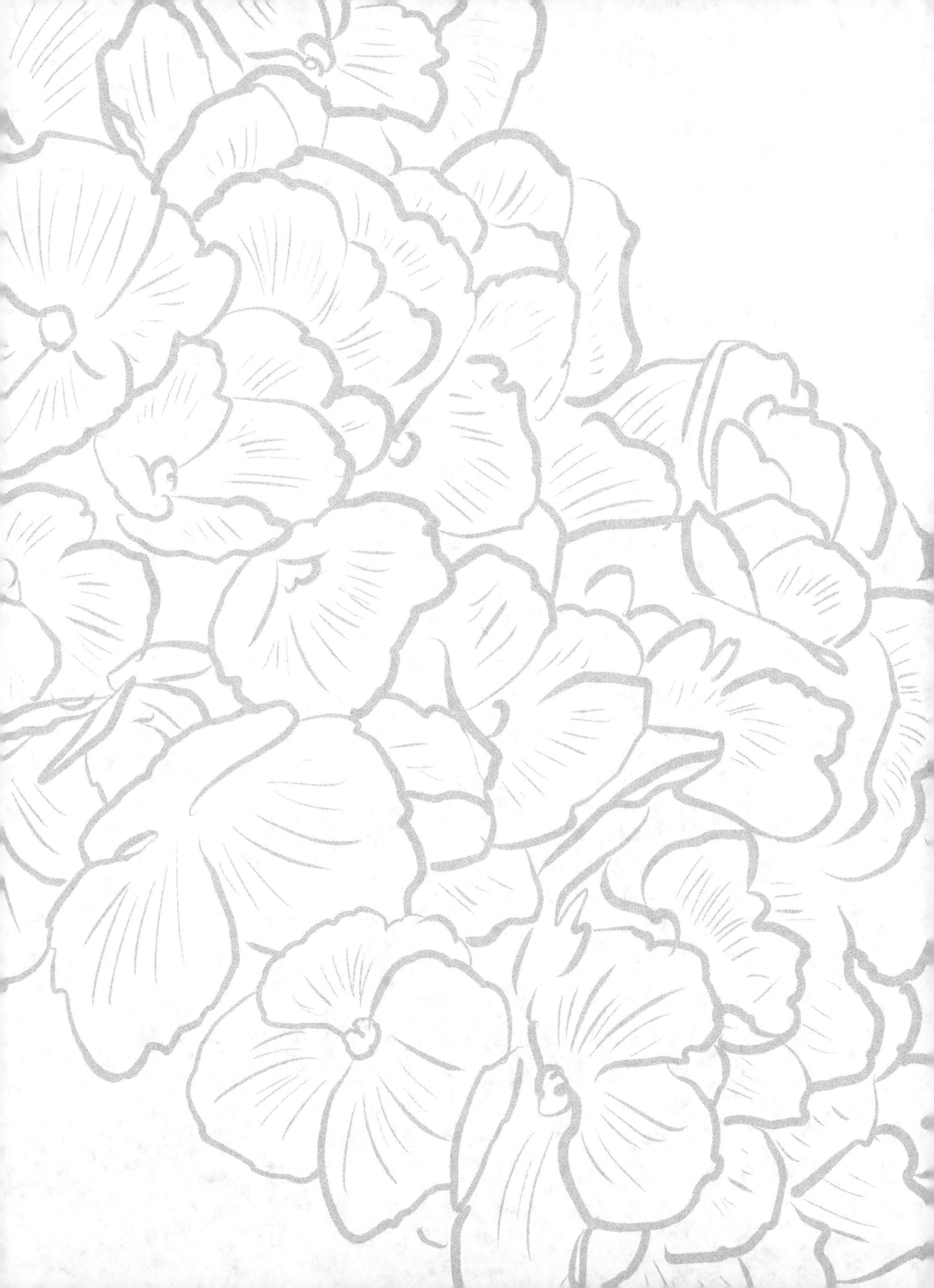

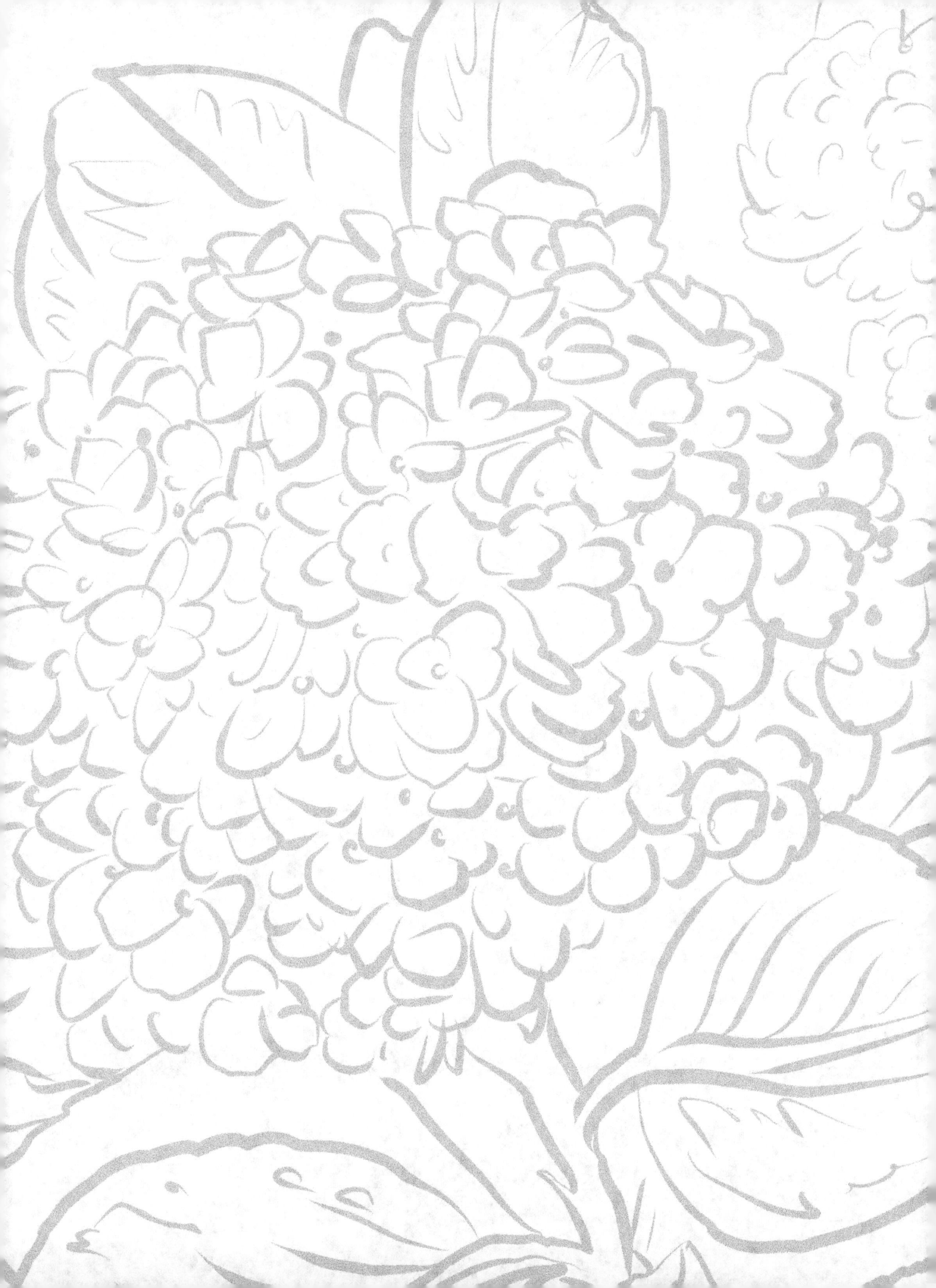

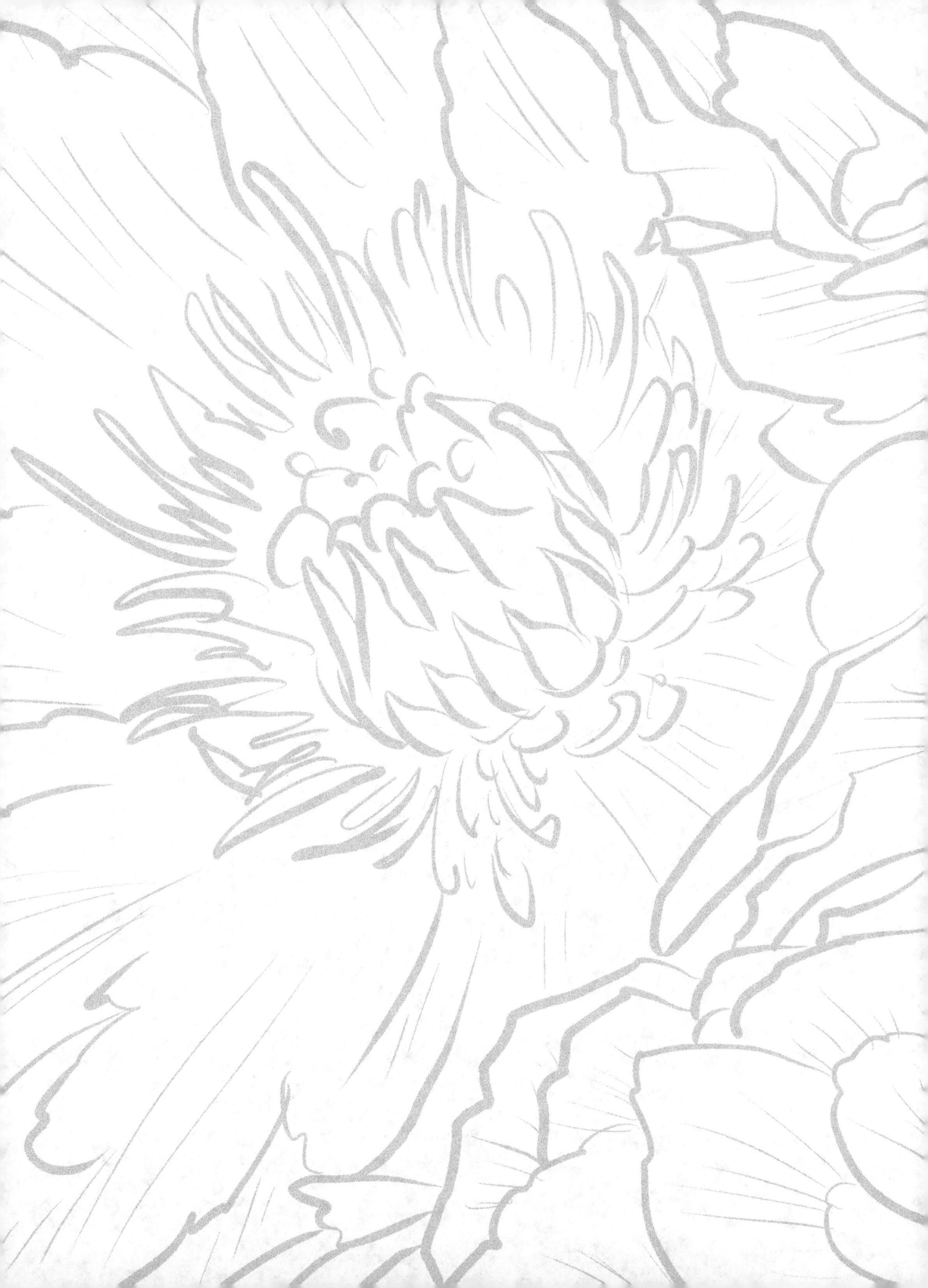

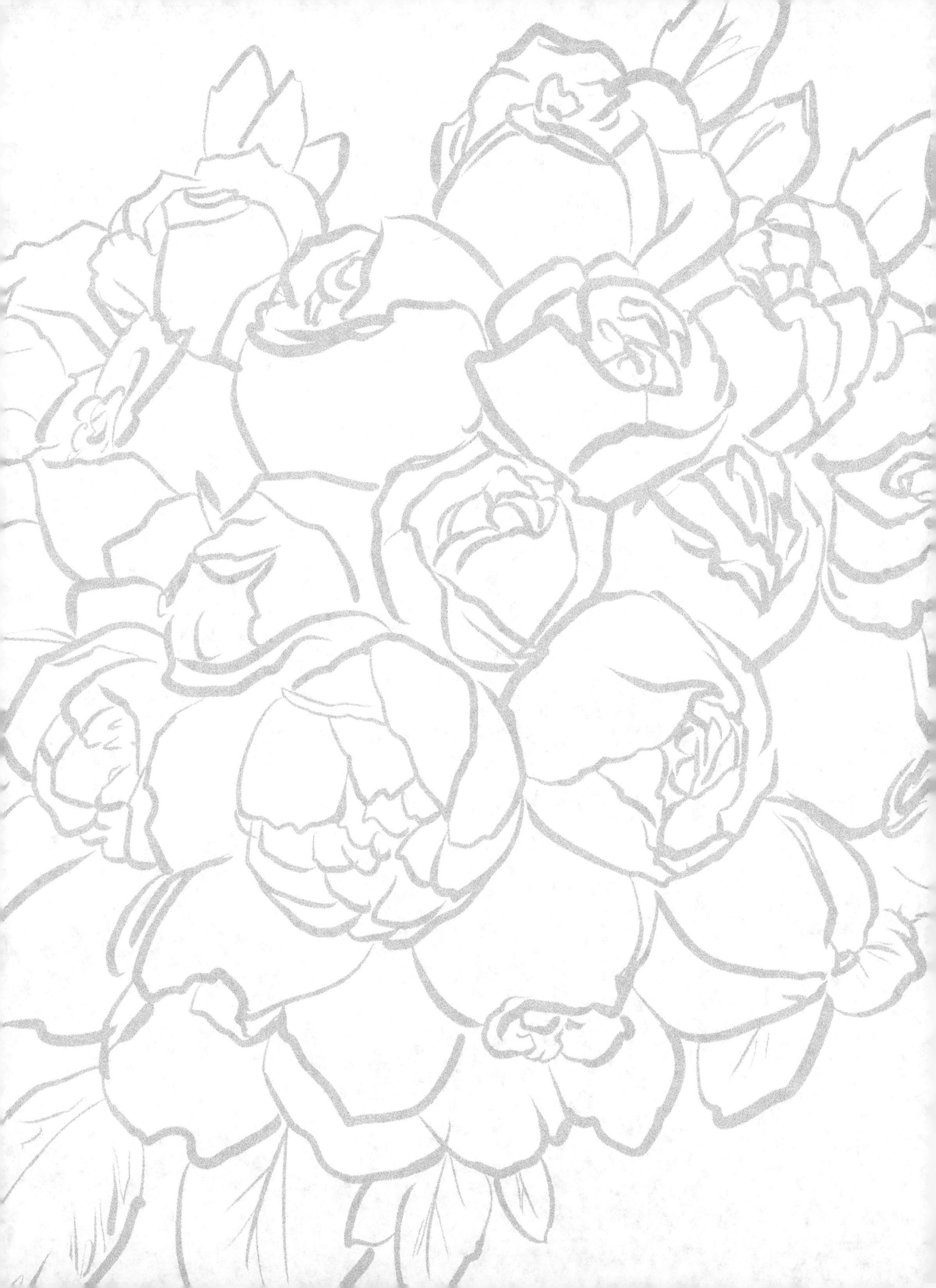

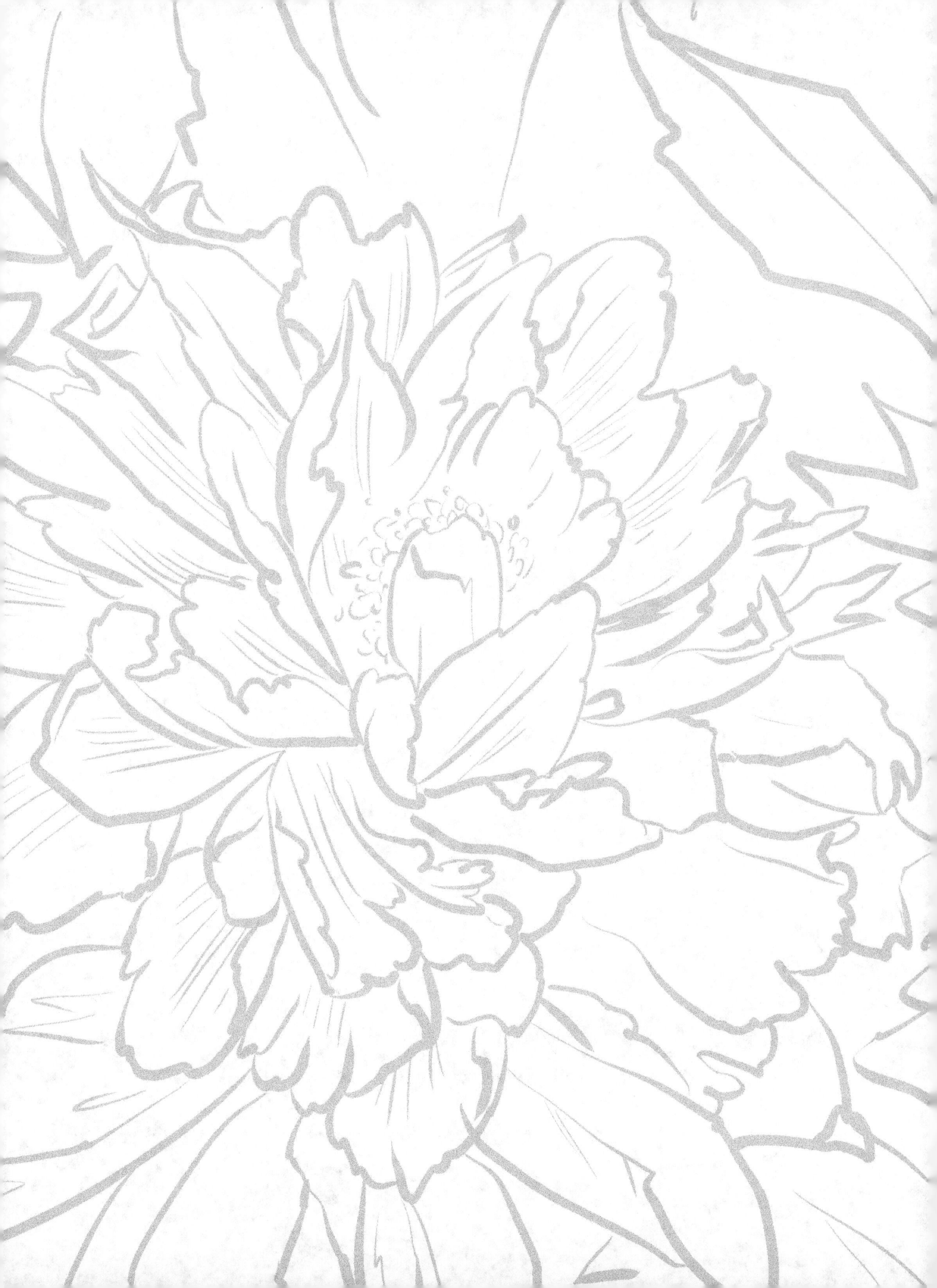